A NEW APPROACH TO COLOSSIANS

A New Approach to Colossians

By

L. J. BAGGOTT

*Canon Residentiary of Norwich Cathedral
and Archdeacon of Norfolk*

LONDON
A. R. MOWBRAY & Co LIMITED

First published in 1961

PRINTED IN GREAT BRITAIN BY
A. R. MOWBRAY & CO. LIMITED IN THE CITY OF OXFORD
0723

FOREWORD

THERE can be little doubt that if the Christian Faith is to gain acceptance in this Nuclear Age, *its oneness with the Creation* must be shown, and all suspicion of disharmony with modern scientific thought removed. Furthermore, the religion to which we are called in Christ must be seen to be such as manifests the human Ideal and makes its attainment possible for all, individually and corporately, for time and for eternity.

The teaching of the Epistle to the Colossions offers a basis for such a presentation of the profoundest Christian truths in which Christ and all that was done and is yet to be done in and through Him are carried back to the Creation of the World and to God's Eternal Purpose therein, and that in Jesus we find the perfect revelation of the mystery of human life and destiny; the creative and educative action of God in Nature and in Man. Similarly, it is the Christian claim that in this Pauline thesis we discover what Jesus means to us to-day; what the Church is meant to be; what the Christian 'hope of Glory' is; and how the Divine Thought and Eternal Purpose of God in Creation and Redemption will yet be completely fulfilled through the power that dwells in Jesus for its realization.

Now if all this can be shown to be true, then those who can receive it will gain a distinctive revelation which neither Science alone nor Philosophy alone, based as they are on human investigation and speculation, which are being continually met by contrary reasons arising from newly discovered theories, can ever give. But the question is—Is all this true in fact and in substance for ourselves to-day? Is this idea of the Cosmic Christ in harmony with the rapidly increasing knowledge of the Universe which modern scientific research provides? It cannot be gainsaid that for large numbers of young intellectual inquirers Science has taken the place of Religion. Advanced thinkers hold to the psychoanalytic view that religion is merely a collective obsessional neurosis whose ceremonies are its symptoms. Others, older perhaps and less influenced by the complexities of scientific and philosophical thought, seek mental and moral assistance from various forms of

non-Christian Mysticism, or from one or more of the varieties of
the Occult. One of the strangest phenomena of our time is the re-
emergence and revival of Buddhism as a way of thought which
offers a way of escape from materialistic formulations. But for
multitudes of people there is no Way of Life at all in this bewildering
world. Life has merely sunk to the level of banality. And the
Christian Religion is considered to be exhausted, having lost its
appeal, sterile, barren, effete and ineffective.

We, at the beginning of the second half of the twentieth century,
are the legatees of this great Faith. Our task is to examine, criticize,
and re-interpret this Pauline thesis in the light of the contemporary
situation, guided by one dominating principle: that in every aspect
of intellectual enterprise, whether scientific, philosophical, or
theological, the banishment of falsehood and error is essential to
the progress of knowledge and the attainment of Truth. Nothing
less than this was Paul's endeavour as he grappled with the heresies
of his day. He saw that the amazing uniqueness of Jesus could only
be explained in the highest categories which the human mind could
achieve. It was essential to the Christian Faith that the Universe
should be seen as God's universe, and Jesus as its crown and glory,
Lord of all Creation, the Cosmic Christ in whom alone its Divine
Origin and End would be complete.

Is this relevant to the modern situation? What really is Christ's
relation to our Nuclear Age with its moon-rockets and sputniks
circling at incredible speeds in ethereal distances of outer Space?

The purpose of this work is to show that Christ, so far from
being outmoded by modern scientific achievement, or unrelated to
this mysterious Universe, is the only clue to a satisfying interpretation of it.

I am grateful to the Editor of *Life and Work* for his kind permission
to reproduce Mr. David Watson's poem on page 132.

L. J. B.

CONTENTS

A man's Life must be nailed to a cross
either of Thought or Action.

> Winston S. Churchill,
> *My Early Life*, p. 127.

PART I

A STUDY OF THE PAULINE THESIS

A Note on the Translation

THE English translation of the Greek text is by the author of the book, who considers that a modern translation is best suited to a 'new approach' to the Epistle. But for the fuller understanding of those who are more familiar with the Authorized Version, it has been decided to print both versions side by side.

INTRODUCTION

THE HISTORICAL BACKGROUND AND EMERGENCE OF PAUL'S THESIS

THE claim of this book is that St. Paul's Epistle to the Colossians may quite properly be called the Gospel of the Cosmic Christ. Profound in thought, its purpose is to show that the Lord Jesus Christ, so far from being unrelated to this mysterious universe, is the only clue to a satisfying interpretation of it. Written in a time of world decay, when the Roman Empire was reeling to its ruin, it proclaims Christ as the Divine Life which not only created all things, but which holds the worlds together. Paul states this truth not only as a proposition of philosophical thought, but as a vision born of a vivid fellowship with the living Christ Himself.

What, then, is the basis of this high claim, this all-transfiguring faith? Briefly stated it is this—One thing man, in his sanity, dare not think, namely, that the sceptics and cynics have read the meaning of life aright, or that the pure and lofty-minded, heroic and true-hearted, have read it amiss. That way lies madness. Paul not only avoided this ultimate delusion, but he dared, in the face of obloquy, scorn, and persecution, to read the meaning of life and the world both philosophically and prophetically: that is, through what is highest in it as the one sure path to the highest Truth. What, then, is the highest fact of which man has any sure knowledge? Paul claims that it is this—*Christ is the sovereign fact of the universe.* That is Paul's master-claim. In Christ he found the revelation of the Eternal Purpose of the world, the secret of its cohesive power, and the prophecy of its creative ideal.

We must seriously consider the validity of this claim. In such a universe as Materialism (whether purely scientific or dialectical) describes, the life of Jesus Christ, His character and His spirit, would be both impossible and absurd, for there would be nothing in such a universe to inspire it, sustain it, uphold and justify it; indeed it would be an effect without a cause, a stream without a spring, a melody without a motif: in short, an anachronism. Therefore, for Paul, the very fact that this universe produced or at least

3

harboured such a life at all, was the refutation of every philosophy of despair. The fact that out of the darkness such a Face
could shine, such a Person could so live, so love, and so teach in a
manner unique in all human history, became the master-light of
all Paul's seeing and the inspiration of his unconquerable assurance.
The meaning of this fact was no thin theory, but an actual reality,
ceaselessly tested in his own life of storm and stress, of struggle and
triumph. The vision of God-in-Christ unified his own complex
nature, gave it coherence, provided strength in weakness, fortitude
in trial, and victory in defeat. Thus it became his gospel—Christ
the Lord of Creation, Christ the Pleroma, Christ the Fullness of
Perfection.

What is the origin of Paul's claim?

Careful study of the map of Europe and Western Asia reveals the
strategic importance of Asia Minor, a continent thrust into the heart
of the Mediterranean world. Running through that continent is
the great road from the Euphrates to Ephesus, along which Oriental
influences travelled to the Occident. Also along this road Seleucus
Nicator, the legatee of Alexander's Asiatic dominions, built seventy-
five cities, from Seleucia on the Tigris to Laodicea. In the western
section of this great highway, and parallel to it, lies the valley of the
Lycus, and the stream which eventually flows into the Maeander.
Travellers, from Herodotus to the latest travellographer, have
described the exquisite and fantastic scenery, the natural bridges
of gleaming travertine, the grottoes crusted with calcareous deposits
which the combined forces of water and earthquake have created.
In this valley, almost within sight of one another, lay the three
famous cities whose stories intermingle.

(1) *Laodicea*, the metropolis of Phrygia, eclipsing all its rivals in
wealth and glory, founded in honour of the beautiful Laodice,
has obtained for itself, from the letter in the Apocalypse (*Rev.*
3 [15-16]), notoriety for the lukewarmness of its politics and especially
of its Christian faith, 'neither hot nor cold', which unhappy fame
is suggested in the tepid stream which reached her from the hot
springs of Hierapolis.

(2) *Hierapolis*, named *The Holy City* because of the multitude
of its temples, although it is doubtful what particular deity was its

tutelary god. Its coins bear the images of Apollo, of the Ephesian Diana, of Æscupalius, and of Hygeia. Certainly the two last mentioned idols were worshipped in Hierapolis on account of the medicinal springs with which it abounded. There was likewise a *Mephitis*, or opening in the earth here, from which a pestilential vapour issued, which was reputed to kill any animal which happened to breathe in it. But more important than all this, Hierapolis is renowned in Early Church History for its bishop Papias as also for being the birthplace of the slave philosopher Epictetus just four or five years before Paul wrote his letter to the Colossians. It may not be too fanciful to suggest that the young slave boy in the house of his master Epaphroditus might well have treasured snatches of the great Apostle's counsel to the slaves of Phrygia and Asia when he wrote of God dwelling in the human body.

(3) *Colosse*, the subject of our inquiry, to which special attention will be given. Though inferior in rank to Laodicea, Colosse was an influential city, and had a Christian church which perhaps was more considerable than the churches in Laodicea and Hierapolis, on account of the number and quality of its members.

All these towns were well-to-do, drawing their affluence from the surrounding fertile territory, busy with the dye-works which spread far and wide, the fame of the 'glossy blacks' of Laodicea and the 'purples' of Colosse. Growing prosperity, however, often breeds a comfortable indifference to politics and religion alike, or as sometimes happens gives occasion to the emergence of some so-called 'New Thought Movement' among the more leisured class who delight to find something different for their unoccupied minds.

Modern Colosse is, of the three, the most difficult to identify; but it is probably to be discovered in the site of the village Chonai. Earthquakes have wrought havoc with the place, and one feels the force of the Apostle's plea in 1 [23]: 'Be not moved away (*earthquake-stricken*) from the hope of the Gospel.' In the year A.D. 60–61 these cities were devastated by a tremendous earthquake, with terrible loss of life. It is remarkable that Paul makes no other allusion to this great calamity which apparently happened very close to the time when this letter was written, unless, of course, it occurred later. In the centuries before the Christian era Colosse (or Colassae, as it is sometimes written) had been a city of considerable dimension. Herodotus, describing the march of Xerxes' hosts, speaks of Colosse as 'a great city of Phrygia,' and Xenophon in his *Anabasis* speaks of it as a 'populous city, great and prosperous.' By the time of Pliny, however, it had sunk from the proud position of *urbs* to that of *oppidum*, though still described as among the 'celeberrima oppida' of the district. It was at this midway point between fame and decadence when Paul wrote his important letter, and, however well-to-do it had been, was now the least considerable of the cities to which a New Testament letter was addressed. Indeed Colosse was by this time somewhat of a backward-going place. Once it had been populous and proud; but ten miles away two other cities had sprung up and sucked its life away. Laodicea had largely captured the trade, and the law-courts had followed, making it the immensely prosperous capital of the province; and across the valley from Laodicea, on a sunny shelf, stood Hierapolis with its hot springs (like those away at Bath in the far-off West Country) to which the doctors of the day sent their wealthy patients, thus making it a fashionable resort. There was much coming and going between the three towns, so that it was easy for Paul's friend Epaphras to minister to all of them. Colosse, however, was rapidly becoming the un-prosperous sister, where the people lived largely on tradition.

The immediate cause of Paul's letter was of considerable impor-tance. Like other cities in pro-consular Asia, selected as representa-tive in the Apocalypse, Colosse had unusual significance: it was the meeting-point of East and West. It stood on the most important route of commerce and intercourse in the eastern part of the Roman Empire; it was, therefore, a place where new ideas and new thoughts were always simmering. As epidemics are said to follow the course of the wind, so false teaching follows the course of the road. The Colossians were susceptible to any novelty, however erroneous it might be. It was in this region that Roman administra-tion and Greek culture had blended as hardly anywhere else in the Empire, and the organized paganism of the west was revealed in what was best as also in what was worst. Here, too, was a very large Jewish population, since to this neighbourhood Antiochus the Great had forcibly conveyed no fewer than two thousand families from Babylonia; a movement which was possibly in Paul's mind when he spoke of God as having 'translated us into the Kingdom of the Son of His love' (1 13). Here also had come the elusive specula-tions of the Orient to fight for a place among the official cults. The

Colossians took a genteel interest in philosophy, leaning to something of an ascetic rigour which suited their small incomes. They were highly developed in mind, and, according to Professor Ramsay, had 'the finest education which the Greek system had developed.' They failed, however, as many do to realize how necessary it is to recognize the radically irreligious nature of pure intellect, though it is seldom honestly avowed. What Paul desired for them was a *consecrated* intellect. Hence the coming of Christianity to such a region constituted a challenge of which the results were to be momentous.

How did the Christian Gospel first reach Colosse?

The inhabitants of Phrygia were famous for the worship of Bacchus, and of Cybele, the mother of the gods. Hence she was called *Phrygia mater* by way of distinction. In her worship, as in that of Bacchus, men and women practised the most shocking debaucheries both in speech and action with a 'frantic rage' which they pretended was occasioned by the 'inspiration of the deities' whom they worshipped. These were the *orgies* (ὀργή = rage) of Bacchus and Cybele, so famed in antiquity, lewd rites which being so perfectly adapted to the corruptions of human nature were lustfully performed by both sexes without shame or remorse. Wherefore, since the Son of God's love came into the world 'to destroy the works of the devil,' it appeared to Paul as a matter of pre-eminent importance to carry the light of the Gospel into the very countries where the devil's works were darkest, and where his abominable impurities were being dignified with the honourable appellation of *religious worship*. It was clear to Paul that nothing but the heaven-descended light of the Gospel could dispel such pernicious infatuation. That this holy purpose might be effectually accomplished, Paul, accompanied by Silas and Timothy, went forth into Phrygia and preached the Gospel with striking success in many cities of that country, as we are informed by St. Luke in his history of the Acts of the Apostles.

Did Paul himself first preach the Gospel at Colosse? Scholars have propounded different views, both affirmative and negative. It is now considered fairly certain that it was not through the personal ministry of Paul that the Christian message first reached the city of Colosse. Paul seems to have come to the cities of the Lycus Valley, not by the main road, but, according to Acts 19 [1], by 'the upper coasts' (ἀνωτερικὰ μέρη). Moreover, the Epistle seems to suggest that the Colossians had not hitherto seen his face (2 [1]). But it seems equally clear that the evangelization of Colosse came about during Paul's two years' residence at Ephesus, when, according to Acts 19 [10], 'all they that dwelt in Asia' heard the word, and when Demetrius complained that the Apostle's doctrine was spread 'almost throughout all Asia.' The great city of the goddess Artemis was strategically chosen to be the centre for missionary effort through-out the province. It is not difficult to suppose that it was at this time Philemon of Colosse 'owed his own soul' to the Apostle; that at this time Archippus was ordained for the work in his native valley; that at this time Trophimus and Tychicus entered the ranks of Paul's fellow-labourers, and that from Ephesus the good man Epaphras set out on a special mission to his city of Colosse. If this is so, then Epaphras (shortened form of Epaphroditus) is the real missionary in the community to which Paul's epistle was eventually sent (cf. 4 [12]: 'Epaphras who is one of yourselves, a servant of Christ, salutes you with his greeting; at all times fervently striving for you by prayers that you may stand fast, perfect and complete, in the whole will of God.') It is this same Epaphras who in course of time arrived at Rome during the Apostle's imprisonment and brought him the comforting news of the faith and love which in general now characterized the Colossian church. But he brought also the gravely disquieting reports which were the immediate cause of the inditing of the letter.

What, then, was the danger which menaced the faith of the Colossian church and so seriously alarmed St. Paul?

If we are to understand the meaning of what is called The Colossian Heresy with which Paul set himself to do vigorous battle, we must first know something of its historical origins; or we shall fail of a true valuation of Paul's majestic answer to it.

The historical origins of the Colossian Heresy

The problem which confronted St. Paul is both age-long and universal. And in no small measure it confronts us to-day. The idea of the creation of the world by a good, wise, beneficent and omni-potent God still presents immense problems not only for theology but also for science and philosophy. While modern science speaks of 'continuous creation' and sees no need for a Creator-God, and philosophy sees the world as a 'Divine Imagining,' theology strives to find solutions not merely to the relation of good and evil which is involved, but more especially to the relation of the Infinite to the Finite. Does it not appear that the self-limitation implied by the contact of the Perfect with the Imperfect, of the Eternal with the Temporal, of the Omniscient with the Ignorant, of the Spiritual with the Material, involves something like a contradiction in terms? Truly the human intellect is faced with immense problems. Yet man has insisted on offering his solutions, and these fall either into the category of some form of Monism or into that of Dualism.

(1) *On the Monistic side* we have (a) first of all the Indian solution which finds ultimate expression in the Upanishads known as the *Vedanta.* Everything here is explained by a categorically monistic idealism which declares that 'there is one only without a second.' According to this theory there is no such thing as creation, only the illusion produced in the soul overspread by ignorance. Deceived by *Māya*, we conceive of the universe as proceeding from the breath of Brahma in prodigious cycles of imaginary evolution, only to be drawn back into its original nothingness at the end of the *Kalpa.* Neither the universe nor we ourselves have any substance of reality. (b) A second form of Oriental monism, less categorical in character, is the Muhammadan mysticism known as Sufism, in which the soul in its quest for fellowship with God finds itself at last absorbed in the Absolute. To many of the Sufic poets of Persia, possibly influenced by Vedantism, there is only one reality, namely God.

(2) *On the side of Dualism* we have a whole chain of systems in close historic contact. (a) Earliest of all is the old Babylonian, or even older Sumerian, system which laid the foundation for all the dualisms which flourished subsequently in the valley of the Euphrates. With the spectacle constantly before their eyes, at the head of the Persian Gulf, of the geological process whereby the struggle of sea and land created alluvial tracts such as gave civiliza-tion a foothold, men found it easy to mythologize. What more natural than to conceive of Marduk, son of the sky-god, lord of the

B

solar ray, chief deity in the Babylonian Pantheon, as coming forth
to war with that horrible monster Tiamât (Hebrew *tehom*), the
horrid goddess of Chaos, of disorder and darkness? It was no
less natural to translate creed into religion by rearing the storied
ziggurats by means of which men might climb through the spheres
of sun and moon and the five planets to fellowship with God-most-
High. (b) On this Babylonian foundation Zoroastrianism built,
superseding the sky-god Anu with Ahura-mazda, the Lord of
Wisdom, turning Tiamât or Chaos into Angra-mainyu the Counterworker, and replacing the planetary gods with the Amesha-spentas
or seven spirits of Ahura-mazda. Then the story of creation is the
story of the making of the 'Sixteen Good Lands' by Ahura-mazda,
followed up and parodied by Angra-mainyu, who is all evil. As
in Rudyard Kipling's fragment entitled *The Seven Nights of Creation*,
no sooner does Ahura-mazda complete a stage of his perfect work
than the Counterworker appears on the scene to mar and frustrate
the labour. Only dimly did the Zoroastrian discern any satisfactory
end, through the coming of Sosiosh, to so desperate and prolonged
a conflict. (c) It is obvious that the various forms of Gnosticism
from their earliest manifestation, discernible in the pre-Christian
Gnostic sects which are represented in Palestine by the Essenes and
the Simonians associated traditionally with the name of Simon
Magus, to the developed systems of Basilides and Valentinus—
and in modern systems of thought of Boehme and Schelling—owe
much to the Persian faith, though it is obvious that attempts were
made to Christianize the general theory. In its more developed
form, which belongs to the post-Pauline period, it strove to attain
a solution to the problem of God in His relation to other beings;
of the creation or genesis of the material world, in which evil is
inherent and therefore antagonistic to God; of the emancipation or
redemption from evil of the spiritual or higher nature of man who,
in his mortal existence, is subject to the power of evil. In his search
for the solution of this highly complex problem, the Gnostic, in
the syncretistic spirit of the age, drew on Greek philosophy and
oriental thought and religion, particularly the Mystery Cults which
professed, by means of a symbolic ritual, to initiate their votaries
into this higher or esoteric knowledge and enable them to attain
thereby the emancipation, the deification of the spirit and its union
with God. Hence the supreme importance of Gnosis, knowledge,

wisdom, from the ethical and philosophical point of view. In the Gnostic theory creation is the result of a series of emanations of semi-divine or divine beings, and, sometimes all emanations, sometimes only the last, the *Demiurgus* who came to be considered as the Creator of the material, inherently evil, world. The Christ is variously interpreted, but always as falling short of that pre-eminence and dignity assigned to Him in the New Testament. Men still have to climb painfully upwards through planetary spheres, as in the Zoroastrian book of *Arda Viraf*, like Muhammad in the *Night Ride*, or like Dante in the *Paradiso*.

The Gnostic world-rulers, however, have now become the Seven Orders: Angels, Archangels, Principalities, Powers, Virtues, Dominions, Thrones. The fundamental idea throughout is that God is necessarily remote from Matter as from an evil thing, and man is still dependent upon the assistance of some lesser god. Hence, finally, in its lower popular form, the resort to magic, astrology and the like, in order either to frustrate the demonic power of evil or to placate the good.

(d) A little later, in the third century A.D., appeared that strange eclectic system known as Manichaeanism which came so dangerously near to being a world-religion, the system whose catechisms were taught from North Africa to China, whose martyrs were burned at York and Orleans, as well as flayed alive in Persia, whose teachings were only suppressed in fire and blood in the massacre of the Albigenses of the thirteenth century. To the Manichaean there was one long frontier between the kingdom of light and the kingdom of darkness. For ages the powers of darkness fought only among themselves, but one day they looked on the light and, hating it, resolved to overcome it. Accordingly a monstrous being called *Satan* was created and led his forces into the realm of light. God, unwilling to send against the evil invader any higher being, created man to repel the raid, with the alarming result that man, insufficiently equipped for the task, was completely defeated, and thereupon became entangled with the darkness. Then God created the present world to be the place of combat between the powers of light and darkness, to endure till the last particle of spirit had been rescued from its capivity.

Thus the great system of the planets was supposed to move like an Oriental water-wheel, each planet like a bucket designed to bring up the *redeemed* element from the dark and discharge it into the column of glory. When at length the work shall have been accomplished, the earth is to be destroyed by fire and the eternal frontier between the light and the dark established for ever.

(e) *Some Modern Aspects of these ideas.* Echoes of the old voices still sound in the ears of men, and Tennyson himself is said to have been at times disposed to accept the philosophy he has put upon the lips of the dying Arthur:

> I found Him in the shining of the stars,
> I marked Him in the flowering of His fields,
> But in His ways with men I find Him not.
> I waged His wars and now I pass and die.
>
> O me! for why is all around us here
> As if some lesser god had made the world
> But had not power to shape it as he would,
> Till the high God behold it from afar,
> And enter it and make it beautiful.

In general it may be said that all forms of error due to defection from the Christian doctrine of the Incarnation swing either in the direction of the Monism which obliterates distinctions between God and the world, or else in the direction of the Dualism which imposes eternal barriers between. On the one side, we see the danger of Mysticism which craves, instead of true fellowship with God, 'to lose ourselves' in the ocean of Divine Love. On the other side is the Calvinism which leaves whole regions of the universe for ever unreconciled to God by the Incarnate Christ.

Among the most distinguished of these modern developments of thought are the works of Boehme, Schelling, and Flournoy.[1]

[1] To deal with these in detail would take us beyond the scope of this book. The serious student, however, may profitably consult the following works:

(i) for Boehme—art. by G. W. Allen: Encyl. of Religion and Ethics.
(ii) for Schelling—J. Watson: Schelling's Transcendental Idealism (1882).
M. Losacco: Schelling (Milano, 1914).
K. Leese: Von Jakob Böhme zu Schelling (Erfurt, 1927).
H. Knittermeyer: Schelling und die Romantische Schule (Munich, 1929).
(iii) for Flournoy—his own work *Le Génie Religieux*, in which he reaches this conclusion: 'If God exists, He has been from the beginning in conflict with some independent Principle whence Evil is derived. He is therefore not the Absolute, the All-powerful, the omnipotent Creator of this Universe; and we must revert inevitably to the ancient Manichaean doctrine.'

The Problem as Paul saw it

Against all such errors, outside and within the Christian fold, Paul lifts up in his Epistle to the Colossians one clear and all-sufficing answer in the doctrine of the Incarnation as it has come to him by revelation and the experience of grace. This we shall endeavour to elucidate as we proceed with our study of the Epistle itself. In the meantime it will suffice to recognize the immense challenge which Christianity flung in the presence of all who demanded an intelligible cosmos. As Professor Santayana has declared: 'Had the Gnostic or Manichaean heresies been victorious, Christianity would have been reduced to a floating speculation.' This St. Paul perceived, and leaped into the fray. Thus, (i) where Gnosticism made Matter the antipodes of God, the Apostle sets forth the Incarnation as bringing God out of remoteness into Matter itself. (ii) Where Gnosticism made of Matter the realm of Evil, the Incarnation is shown to reveal it as the very Body of God. (iii) Where Gnosticism made Matter an obstacle to progress, the Incarnation manifested it as the sacramental medium through which God approaches the human soul. (iv) Where Gnosticism required a chain of principalities and powers by means of which a man might climb up to God, the Incarnation proclaims an ever-present and all-sufficient Mediator, bone of our bone, and flesh of our flesh, at once Son of Man and Son of God. (v) Where Gnosticism made of creation a degrading and defiling thing, Paul's Christian doctrine reveals it as the very climax of Divine Love, the perfecting of the Divine existence by participation in the experience of the finite, even as it is also the prophecy of the completing of human existence by man's participation in the infinite. In a word, God is our closest companion in all the pilgrimage and struggle of life.

Much has been written with reference to the Colossian Heresy, and the question has been debated at length as to whether the heresy was Jewish or pagan, strictly so-called. We may safely say that it was both. The presence of Jewish elements in the errors of Colosse is clear from the reference to formalism. Certain false teachers had persuaded some of the Colossian Christians to worship Angels, to abstain from animal food, to observe the Jewish festivals, new moons and sabbaths, and to mortify their bodies by long continued fastings: in short, to practise the rites and restrictions of the law of

Moses as absolutely necessary to their salvation (2 [16-23]). But it
should be noted that the formalism here denounced by Paul is
no longer that of the Galatians, dictated by the desire to make
righteousness perfect through the Law; it is rather the result of an
ascetic determination to subdue the flesh to the spirit and so attain
freedom from the bondage to Matter. But this spirit of asceticism,
through which regard to the Law is enjoined and such rules as 'taste
not, touch not, handle not' enforced, is in itself foreign to pure
Judaism. It is nothing else but that protean form of Oriental
philosophy, due to the super-imposition of Zoroastrian dualism
upon the old Babylonian worship of the Seven Planetary Gods—
sun, moon, and five planets, still suggested in the names of the days
of the week. There is no need (with Bp. Lightfoot) to call it strictly
Essenism, although Palestinian Essenism, such as is alluded to by
Pliny and Josephus and largely confirmed by the discovery of the
Dead Sea Scrolls, was doubtless influenced by similar contacts with
the Orient. Nor need we call it strictly Gnosticism, although the
Gnostic systems are developed under similar circumstances. It is
one attempt among many to nullify the essential message of Christianity by substituting for that message a syncretism of Jewish and
pagan ideas.

Since we are considering Paul's letter from a philosophical angle,
let us examine the philosophical side of this particular question.
(i) The fundamental intellectual difficulty which confronted men,
then as to-day, was how to reconcile the absolutism of God with
the act of creation. Did God create the world out of nothing?
If so, then the statement was equivalent to the assertion that all things
proceeded out of Himself. Consequently, the problem of evil,
out of which—with the granting of freedom to the human will—
sprang the problem of sin, was obviously due to God Himself; and
God must therefore be regarded as the author of evil. From this
logical conclusion men revolted. (ii) Hence arose the disposition
to assign evil to a separate order of things, and so, in one form or
another, to establish a categorical dualism. The identification of the
evil half of this dualism with *Hyle* or Matter, brought back the first
problem in another form. How could the infinite God, the Lord
of the spirit, come into touch with Matter in such a way as to be,
in any real sense of the word, Creator of all things 'visible and
invisible'? In two ways, it was replied: (a) either by a series of *falls*

on the part of Deity in which the passion of God involved Him
in the material and evil realm, or (b) by the sending forth of a number
of *æons* or emanations which should eventually establish contact
with the world of Matter. Thus, as in the old Babylonian ziggurat-
worship, God was supposed to project His presence downward
to men through the Seven Planetary Gods, and men in return were
thought to reach up to God by the aid of these intervening 'principalities and powers'. Thus God and man became remotely and
indirectly related. (iii) The antagonism thus postulated between
Spirit and Matter, between Infinite and Finite, led inevitably to
serious errors both theological and practical.

On the theological side it induced the worship of beings who were
supposed to be intermediate between Man and God, 'world-rulers'
(κοσμοκράτορες) as Paul calls them, arranged in a mystical hierarchy
of Angels, Archangels, Thrones, Dominions, Virtues, Principalities,
Powers. This was surely to dethrone Christ from His place as the
'one Mediator.' Furthermore, long before the light of the Christian
Gospel shone on the world, the Greeks had introduced their philosophy into many of the countries of Asia Minor, and among the rest
into Phrygia where the doctrines of Pythagoras and Plato were
much admired. The followers of Plato held that the government
of the world is carried on by beings inferior to the gods, but superior
to men, such as, in their turn, the Jews believed Angels to be.
These they called Δαίμονες or *Divinities*: and these they enjoined
their sect to worship on account of their agency in human affairs.

On the practical side there was the disposition to separate men into
the two categories of Spiritual (ψυχικόι) and Material (ὑλικόι),
with a curious divergent result. On the one hand, men imposed
upon themselves all kinds of ascetic restrictions: 'Touch not, taste
not, handle not'; and, on the other hand, they plunged with equal
fanaticism into every excess of carnal licence. On the one hand,
they sought to rise to things spiritual by extreme mortification of
the flesh; on the other hand, they regarded Matter as so inherently
and so hopelessly evil that it mattered not at all into what depths
of mire the flesh was flung.

The philosophy of Pythagoras led to a different discipline. It
was held that mankind had all lived in some pre-existent state, and
that for the sins previously committed by them, some of their souls
were sent into human bodies, and others of them into the bodies of

brutes, to be punished for and purged from their former sins. Believing that the whole brute creation was thus animated by human souls, they held it unlawful to kill anything which had life, and therefore imperative to abstain wholly from animal food. Thus, to free themselves effectually from the vices and pollutions contracted in their pre-existent condition, they practised repeated and pro-longed fastings and other severities for the purpose of a thorough-going subjection of the body (with all its appetites and lusts) to the soul. On the other hand, the Judaizers who came to Colosse, the more effectually to recommend the law of Moses to the Christians of that city, affirmed that Pythagoras derived his disciplines, and Plato his dogmas, from the writings of Moses. That these false teachers who were busy sowing the seeds of heresy made use of an argument of this kind, to recommend the Jewish institutions to the Colossians, as the more profitable, that some of the early Christian writers together with some of the Jewish writers also in the first ages, affirmed the very same fact. It cannot be denied that the Pythagorean discipline bears some resemblance to the abstinence from unclean meats, and to the fastings enjoined in the law of Moses. But it is perfectly clear that the Pythagorean precepts concerning both abstinence from animal food and the mortifying of the body by fasting and other severities, together with the Platonic doctrine concerning the agency of angels in human affairs, and the honour that is due to them from men on that account, are all expressly condemned by the Apostle in his Epistle to the Colossians. These Judaizing teachers, artfully adapting their tenets to the characters and prejudices of those whom they addressed, lectured the Colossians in a plausible and pompous manner concerning the dignity and office of angels, representing them as proper objects of worship to mankind on account of the manifold blessings which they received through their ministry, and even insinuated that, to render mankind complete in knowledge, new and more illu-minating revelations of God's will, infinitely more perfect than anything made by Christ, might the more properly be expected through their ministry since angels were far better acquainted with God's will than it was even remotely possible for Christ to be, since Christ was nothing but a man. Indeed they further claimed that their own doctrines were such revelations so mediated. Further-more, was not the law of Moses given by the ministry of angels?

Did not angels conduct the Israelites into Canaan? With respect to such of the Colossians as were tinctured with the Platonic philosophy, in order to persuade them to worship angels or at least to honour their mediation in worshipping God, they affirmed that it was intolerable arrogance in sinners to worship God without some mediator, and therefore they exhorted these Colossians, as an exercise of humility becoming them, to utter their prayers to the Almighty by the instrumentality of angels, such prayers being the more acceptable to God, more certain to reach Him, and more effectual therefore than any mediation of Christ who, being human, could not reasonably be held, expected, or supposed to have any power at all with God, since God's angels are His ministers in the government of the world.

But what of propitiation of sin by sacrifice? Was not this even more effectual? Yes indeed, said the Judaizers; but since there were no propitiatory sacrifices prescribed in the Gospel, it was undoubtedly the will of God to continue the sacrifices and purifications of the law of Moses, which He Himself had appointed as the means of procuring remission of sins. Therefore the Colossians must embrace the Mosaic law as an institution excellently calculated, and Divinely established, for procuring the pardon of offences, and for perfecting men in virtue, and therefore absolutely essential for salvation.

Here, then, we have in brief the danger which Paul set himself steadfastly to face, with infallible and inspired instinct. He perceived that the worship of these Christians in Asia was being given to angels rather than to Christ, and that their morals were being swayed by alternate tides of asceticism and antinomianism. The subsequent history of the communities in the Lycus valley affords still further illustration of the danger. It is this which gives such point to the warnings of the Seer concerning the danger of angel-worship in the Apocalypse (Rev. 22 [9]). It is also further illustrated in the history of Cerinthus, related by Polycarp and reported by Irenaeus and Eusebius. Well might St. John hesitate to greet as a brother one whose theology made the God of the Jews only an Angel, a Demiurgus or Underworker, such as Plato had spoken of in the *Timaeus*, and whose Christology reduced the Christ to the position of the temporary tabernacle of the *Pleroma* or Fullness. Moreover, in the light of the Epistle to the Colossians, we understand more clearly the significance of the frequent dedication of local Churches to angels and archangels. We read between the lines of the story told by a native of Colosse, Nicetas of Chonium, how the archangel Michael saved the Colossians from the waters of an inundation by breaking a passage through at the chasm where, in memory of the event, was erected 'The Church of the Archangel.'

An outline of Paul's argument

To the above-mentioned form of doctrine, by drawing men away from Christ the Head and making them forfeit all the benefit which flows from His mediation, it was necessary that an effectual remedy should be provided for bringing to an end so pernicious a scheme of error. And Paul realized that the remedy for doctrinal error is sound theology. Such a remedy St. Paul provides in this remarkable Epistle in which all the errors of the false teachers are not only condemned but sound contrary truths established. In particular, the Levitical sacrifices and purifications were shown by the Gospel to be useless, 1 [14], 'That we have redemption through the sacrifice of Christ, even the forgiveness of sins.' Likewise, with regard to the figment that angels are superior in dignity and power to Christ; 1 [15]; that Christ 'is the image of the invisible God, the firstborn or Lord of the whole creation'; verse 16: 'Because by Him were created all things which are in the heavens and upon the earth, things visible and invisible, whether they be thrones or lordships' etc.; consequently, that the angels themselves, whatever the nature of their office in the universe may be, were created by Christ, and are completely subject to Him; verse 18: 'That He is the Head, or ruler of the body, even of the Church'; verse 19: 'For it pleased the Father that in Him *all the fullness of perfection and power* should continually dwell'; accordingly, that the Colossians had no valid inducement to worship either evil angels through fear or good angels through humility. Therefore, to put these doctrines concerning the dignity and office of Christ beyond all doubt, Paul told the Colossians, 1 [25-26], that he was commissioned by God Himself to preach them to the whole world.

Next, because the false teachers insinuated that a more perfect revelation of the will of God might be expected through the

ministry of angels than that which Christ had made, the Apostle
assured the Colossians, 2 ⁸, 'That in Him all the treasures of wisdom
are laid up,' and added, verse 4, 'This I affirm that no one may
deceive you with plausible speech' concerning the office and power
of angels in the government of the world. He therefore ordered
them, verse 8, 'to take care that no one made a prey of them,
through an empty and deceitful philosophy,' namely the Platonic
philosophy in which the dignity and office of angels were so highly
extolled; because, verse 9, 'In Christ continually dwelleth all the
fullness of the Godhead bodily.' Also, because the Judaizers endeavoured to persuade such of the Colossians as were tinctured
with the Pythagorean philosophy, to receive the precepts of the law
of Moses concerning meats and fastings, as conformable to the
Pythagorean precepts, and as having the same influence to purify
the soul; the Apostle told them that they had no need either of the
Platonic dogmas concerning angels or the Pythagorean precepts
about abstinence, because, verse 10, 'they were made complete
in everything necessary to their sanctification and salvation by the
precepts, mediation, and government of Him who is the Head of all
government and power.' Further, because the Judaizers extolled
the sacrifices and purifications appointed in the law of Moses as
the only effectual means of obtaining the pardon of sin, Paul
assures them that these were now completely outmoded and utterly
useless, because, verse 14, Christ by His death had 'blotted out the
handwriting of ordinances contained in the Law with its curse,
and had nailed it to His cross in its blotted-out state, that all might
see clearly that the curse of the Law was removed.' He accordingly
ordered them to resist every teacher who attempted to impose
upon them either the ordinances of the law of Moses or the Pythagorean abstinences and mortifications, verse 16, 'Let no one rule
you in meat or in drink or in respect of a festival or of a new moon
or of sabbaths.' And in relation to the worshipping of angels as
more powerful mediators than Christ, he said to them, verse 18:
'Let no teacher make you lose your reward, delighting in humility
and the worship of angels, verse 19, and not holding the Head,'
plainly instructing the Colossians that in praying to God, if they
made use of the mediation of angels on pretence of humble
approach, and worshipped them as the authors of the blessings
which they enjoyed, they renounced Christ the Head and deprived

themselves of the benefits of His own personal mediation, thus losing all the blessings they were entitled to, as members of His Body.

In order to make the Colossians still more sensible of their folly in listening to the false teachers, Paul asked them, verse 20, 'Since ye have died with Christ from the elements of the world,' that is, since you have been freed by your dying with Christ both from the heathen philosophy and the deplorably superstitious observances connected with the worship of the astral powers and from the Mosaic law, why as living under that philosophy and law do you subject yourselves to their ordinances, which things are not according to the commandments of God, but, verse 22, 'according to the commandments of men?' Besides, verse 23, though these commandments have the appearance of Gnosis or wisdom, they are in reality unmitigated foolishness, being destructive of the vigour both of mind and body.

In 2 [18] Paul may be thinking especially of one particular sect of the Jews, namely, the Essenes. What he mentions, verse 23, of the *neglecting* of the body, so a similar regard in Essenism concerns a *caring* for the angels. This we learn from Josephus (*De bello Judaic.* lib. 2, c. 7, sive 12) that when the Essenes received any into their number, they required the taking of a solemn oath, 'That they would keep or observe the books of their sect, and the names of the angels, with like care.' It is difficult to say why the Essenes took such care of the names of angels. Did they make use of them in their charms to cure diseases? Did they in fact pay them such worship as Paul condemns, 2 [18]? The other things condemned by Paul are certainly theirs, and agree to the Essenes above all others.

The immense care with which Paul here taught the creation of all things by God's beloved Son, 1 [15-17], doubtless proceeded from his observation of the beginnings of the absurd notion that the world was made by an evil principle, which was first broached in the Christian Church by the Gnostics and further propagated by their disciples, the Marcionites, Encratites, and Manichaeans; or at least it proceeded from Paul's insight into the possibilities concerning the rise and progress of the gravely damaging tenets of these heretics, all flowing from their doctrine of creation by an evil principle; and his anxiety to guard the faithful against such pernicious errors. Although Paul's philosophy of creation and the world in general has been described by notable scholars as 'pessimistic and undoubtedly Gnostic,' Paul's hope is not in the world at all, but in Him who created the world and who redeemed it from the evil that had infected and disrupted it. His philosophy is centred in Christ, the pre-existent Christ as the predetermined agent of God's purpose. Evil is the work of Satan and strange astral powers which dominate the universe and man; it takes possession of both in the downfall of Adam. But Christ becomes incarnate, the second Adam, the sinless embodiment in human life of all that the first Adam should have been but failed to be. He is the predetermined Redeemer through whom the Divine Grace operates unto justification from sin, death and condemnation. Such is the redemptive purpose of God for man and also for the universe likewise afflicted with sin.

But not only were these heretics teaching a cosmogony grounded in evil, but in order to overcome that evil it was essential to weaken and subdue the body as the fountain of all human depravity, by every form of discipline and hardship; and since wine and marriage tended to bodily gratifications, they must be wholly rejected in order that the mind might be freed from the fetters and contagions of Matter. Hence the distinction between the Gnostic or spiritually superior class which alone is capable of the 'higher' knowledge, therefore of the 'higher' life of the spiritual superman (πνευματικοί), and the inferior natural class (ψυχικοί or σαρκικοί), which cannot rise to such noble heights but can only strive to do so imperfectly and inavailingly. Hence the austerities which the Marcionites, Encratites, Manichaeans and others practised.

However, not all such heretics were like-minded: some were inclined to sensual excesses, claiming the support of the same dogmas concerning the natural pravity of Matter as the basis of the cosmic evil principle, and accordingly took to themselves a liberty of gratifying their lusts without fear; for they affirmed that *piety* consists alone in the knowledge of God and in the union of mind with Him; and that they who attain this union, and by contemplation draw their minds away from their body have no concern at all with the actions of the body, and are therefore under no obligation to restrain its natural propensities. Hence proceeded the abominably dissolute lives of the Carpocratians and others who affirmed that all things were lawful to them, and that temperance was enjoined to men not by God but by the maker of the world, an evil being.

Of this twofold discipline, proceeding from one and the same source, there are many traces in scripture. Among the first corrupters of Christianity Paul mentions some who arrogate to themselves a great show of wisdom by a voluntary neglect of the body (2 23). And both Peter and Jude speak of others who were so corrupted as to affirm that Christ had purchased for them a liberty of sinning. Lust was lawful (cf. 1 *St. John*). Similarly in the Letter to the Church of the Laodiceans we find clear indications of the errors which the false teachers endeavoured to disseminate in Phrygia. For example, to show that angels are not superior to Christ in dignity and power, and that they are not to be worshipped on account of their ministry in the government of the world, the writer asserts Christ's power as Creator of the world, in terms almost precisely similar to those used by Paul in his Epistle to the Colossians. In Rev. 3 14 Christ is 'the beginning ($\dot{a}\rho\chi\eta$ = the *efficient cause*) of the Creation.' Paul makes full use of Gnostic terminology, such as 'wisdom,' 'mystery,' 'pleroma,' 'the spiritual' in contrast to 'the psychic' or 'natural man,' etc., in order to show how Christ alone provides the true meaning; to set forth the divine purpose of creation and redemption from the evil that clearly affects the universe and every man in it; to assert the whole supremacy of Christ in whom alone, as the historic manifestation of the Divine Purpose, is the true knowledge, gnosis, wisdom, available. He who is the efficient cause of creation is this historic Person, Christ Jesus, in whom all fullness dwells, not in the fictitious phantom of the Gnostic imagination, but in the living embodiment of the redemptive idea and purpose of God.

Again, because the false teachers who troubled the churches of Phrygia were 'puffed up' on account of their assumed knowledge in 'things not seen' (2 18), and thought themselves complete in every respect by obeying the Mosaic precepts and the prescriptions of the heathen philosophy, Christ Himself condemned that vain boasting in the Laodiceans, Rev. 3 17: 'Thou sayest, I am rich and increased with goods, and have need of nothing, and knowest not that thou art wretched and miserable and blind and naked.' In other words, the higher knowledge is to be professed with humility in contrast to Gnostic presumption and vanity. Speculation concerning 'things not seen' is not the same as Christian experience of the exalted Christ.

Heresy dies hard. Although the worship of angels was at first repressed in the churches of Phrygia by Paul's letter to the Colossians, it afterwards prevailed among them to such a degree that the Council which met at Laodicea, A.D. 344, the metropolis of Phrygia, found it necessary to condemn that idolatry by their 35th Canon: 'Christians ought not to leave the church of God, and go and name angels, or gather assemblies. If, therefore, any one is found to practise this secret idolatry, let him be anathema, because he has left our Lord Jesus Christ the Son of God, and has turned to idolatry.' In its last two Canons the Council declared what sacred books were to be publicly read in the churches.

Paul's place in the early history of Christianity

'Paul, an apostle of Christ Jesus through the will of God'—This opening sentence, or in similar words, to all his Epistles may be described as the *Preparatio Evangelica*.

For the understanding of any great literary work two preliminaries are essential: one is that the particular document to be studied should be properly related to the developing mind of the author, and the other is that the writer himself should be properly related to his particular place in the development of the ages. These preliminaries are as essential for the full appreciation of a Biblical work as, for example, of a modern scientific thesis, unless of course we are to regard the books of the Bible as totally unrelated both to the human minds which were the channels of revelation and to the ages of the world in which they first appeared.

One of the most striking of all metaphors used in the Gospels for 'the Kingdom of Heaven' is that of the *Seed*; and the force of the metaphor lies in the fact that, whereas the seed considered in itself as a thing self-contained and separate with a potential life of its own, from the moment it is placed in the soil it begins to be affected by those conditions which qualify its growth. So the Divine Word, committed to Time, must have its secular unfolding, 'first the blade, then the ear, then the full corn in the ear.' The same is true of Christian history regarded as a whole. It is also true of the experience of the individual Christian. With Browning, any Christian soul may find it true

> That one Face, far from vanish, rather grows
> Or decomposes, but to recompose,
> Become my universe and knows.

Yet, this development which we concede both to the whole body
and to the normal individual, has been largely denied, sometimes
tacitly, sometimes explicitly, to the apostolic writers who contributed so large a part of the New Testament scriptures. At least
it is difficult on any other hypothesis to understand the continued
retention of a non-chronological sequence in the case of Paul's
Epistles; which suggests to the general reader that the Pauline
experience was from first to last entirely static. It cannot, however,
be denied that the Apostles advanced in knowledge during the days
of the ministry; or that the Holy Spirit came to lead them into all
truth. Yet, the Holy Spirit having been given, we are prone to
imagine their spiritual and intellectual equipment complete at a
stroke. The counterpart of this would be to expect in Confirmation
a sevenfold gift from which the 'daily increase, more and more'
has been excluded. We ought rather to welcome the doctrine of a
developing Christianity such as includes the apostolic age among the
rest. It would save us many a futile effort to discover fruit out of
season. Indeed, the Forty Years between Pentecost and the Fall of
Jerusalem is as pre-eminently the period of preparation for the
independent life of the Christian Church as the Forty Years in the
Wilderness proved to be the needed time of preparation for the
entrance of Israel upon an independent national existence. These
years should rather be regarded as the pre-natal period of Church
history, even the period in which its life is still bound up with
the life of the mother Church of Judaism. During this generation
we have a threefold development in the direction of a full catholicity.
First, there is the *Geographical* development by missionary expansion
which completes the apostolic witness to the scattered Hebrew
communities. This witness came to Judaism by the year A.D. 70
when the destruction of the changeable led to the revelation of that
four-square City which is the eternal Holy of Holies. Secondly,
there is the *Institutional* development which reveals the organism of
the Body in its ministerial and sacramental order. Thirdly, there is
a *Doctrinal* development which is to issue in a more completely
stated Christology than was possible at first. This, however, is not
to say that all Christian witness of apostolic days was not, from first
to last, Christo-centric. Indeed it was. But to 'grow in the grace
of our Lord Jesus Christ' was also to grow in understanding. As,
serving God with all their hearts, they increased in love; and,

as serving God with all their wills, they ripened in character; so, serving God with all their minds, they increased in intellectual apprehension of the things they taught. Consequently the New Testament Epistles are documents representing, in authorship and time, many varying stages of intellectual experience. In most cases it is not easy to discern the growth which we may nevertheless properly assume. The Epistle of St. James, for example, represents an early stage in which the historic ministry is still of recent memory. Here Christ, though Lord and Master, is less a *cosmic* figure than the moralist, the teacher, and the prophet. The Johannine writings, on the other hand, represent a stage of experience in which the historic has long since faded into a measure of insignificance as compared and contrasted with a spiritual fellowship with Him who is now seen to be nothing less than the *Logos*, the Eternal Word of God. The historical is not forgotten, but is the illustration in Time of absolute and eternal facts related to Christian experience such as no 'life after the flesh' could ever be.

In each of the foregoing cases there is no sufficient material spread over the years from which to trace the mental development of the writer. But in the case of the Pauline Epistles, which extend over a period of at least two decades, we have precisely what is otherwise lacking. The whole of Paul's career, whether considered from the point of view of the missionary or of the writer, is the story of steady, systematic, and continuous advance towards fullness of experience and perfection of expression; yet to the end ever learning in the school of Christ. We see him as a diligent young student at the University of Tarsus which was one of the chief centres of Greek culture. The son of strict Jewish parents and destined to be brought up as a Rabbi, he gained an amazing mastery of Hellenistic Greek which, together with his command of the Rabbinic dialectic and his insight into the Stoic-Platonic philosophy and his knowledge of Graeco-Roman Law, made him an ideal expositor of the Stoic doctrines of the divine immanence, of a natural moral law (which is the Gentile equivalent of the Mosaic law) of conscience as an innate witness to God and 'the good', of human brotherhood, and the like. He clearly understood the Platonic doctrine of the distinction between the visible world and the eternal spiritual reality beyond it, of which it is the reflection, and of the dualism in man and the universe between 'spirit' and 'Matter.' Common

C

to Paul and the current Platonism is the longing for redemption from this material existence with its moral and spiritual limitations, though the actual redemption is markedly different. Furthermore, Paul's Epistles show clear traces of a knowledge of the Greek mystery cults, and from his Epistle to the Colossians it is evident that he was brought into close contact with the religio-philosophic movement later known as Gnosticism, for he uses not only terms characteristic of this form of thought but also claims to be in possession of the true Gnosis, or higher religious philosophy.

It is inadvisable, however, to over-emphasize the Hellenistic influence upon Paul's personal thought, as some scholars have done, since Paul himself seems to have regarded it as essentially antagonistic to the Gospel. Nor did it materially affect his Hebrew predilections. Even on the eve of his conversion when he listened with burning heart to the speech of Stephen, a member of the Jewish-Hellenist synagogue, the bitter opposition which Saul the Pharisee, Jew of the Diaspora, displayed, showed that, at that stage of his spiritual evolution, he was not disposed to tolerate any aberration from the traditions of the Fathers.

We see Paul also at the feet of Rabban Gamaliel at Jerusalem who instructed him 'according to the strict manner of the law of our fathers' (*Acts* 22 ³)[1] by which he obtained that mastery of Rabbinic exegesis of which his Epistles bear ample trace. Indeed his appeal to Scripture is, for Paul, the indispensable proof of the claim of the new faith to be the true religion.

Then came the divine lesson, so humbly received, on the Damascus Road, and, in the following days of silence and darkness, gaining a new conception of the true mission of his race, followed by the patient months of meditation and study in Arabia. It was no accident that it was a Jew of the Diaspora who became the great Apostle of the Gentiles. None was better fitted for the task. To the Greek he became 'a Greek and all things to all men' (1 *Cor.* 9 ²¹⁻²²) in the prosecution of his Christian mission: but he could never have done so without the previous knowledge, experience, learning, and scholarly insight into the Hellenistic environment. Yet Paul cannot be explained as the product of any external influence, or of the complex religious ideas of his age; and although his Christianity may be said to be the product of Hebraism supplemented by Hellen-

[1] For a scholarly account of Rabbinic faith, see Dr. Kohler's *Jewish Theology*.

ism, it was more truly the product of the man himself, of his personal religious experience, especially the supreme experience of his conversion, of the sensitively subtle and powerful intellect which, while making the fullest use of his inherited Jewish thought, gave this thought a wholly new content; of the ethical and spiritual intensity which transformed the fanatical Pharisee into the flaming Apostle of a new Faith, the Prophet of a new spiritual life, and the Philosopher of a new interpretation of the Universe, the greatest creative mind of early Christian history.

Think, too, of the strenuous years of missionary adventure reported for us in the Acts, during which years his vision grew in clearness with every onward step. His one ambition is 'Christ for the world, and the world for Christ': Christ as the Revealer of God and the Redeemer from sin and death under which the whole Creation writhes in pain.

But of all the evidences of vital growth, there is nothing to compare with that revealed in the series of Epistles which have been so providentially preserved for our instruction. Arranged, however, in what appears to be order of length rather than order of time, the Pauline Epistles are for the most part read with little or no appreciation of their developing thought and expanding range. It is difficult to excuse the conservatism which still retains this unhappy order. In the case of the Qūran, the compilers may have had some excuse for placing the *suras* in order of length, because ot their entire ignorance of the proper sequence. It is the same kind of conservatism that refrains from restoring the chronological order of the Old Testament prophecies which modern scholarship has established, in any new issue of the Bible. There is no excuse, however, for keeping New Testament readers in the dark as to the correct sequence of Paul's letters, for as things are we miss both the gradual unfolding of his vision and the advancing power of his unique teaching faculty.

The Four Groups of Pauline Letters. Let us then, at the outset of our study, recall the contents of the four groups of letters which the Christian Church has agreed to accept as the genuine product of Paul's pen, although a number of critics are still at variance over the genuineness of the Epistles to the Ephesians, 2 Thessalonians, Timothy, and Titus, since they show what is considered to be the influence of post-Pauline thought and ecclesiastical development.

(1) First, about the time of the second missionary journey, we have the two Thessalonian epistles (c. A.D. 52), on questions mainly of local, domestic, and temporary interest, consisting of Paul's ordinary theological and ethical counsels designed to steady the faith of the Christian community in the presence of millennial expectations of the cruder sort. It is not quite clear that Paul himself did not at this time share in some form of this expectation. The most marked feature of his theology in this group is—Jesus is the Lord, the Christ, the Son of God, the Judge of men. All rule and all authority is in His name. Christ is divine, equal with the Father.

(2) Secondly, from the third missionary journey, we have the Epistles of the Judaeo-Christian controversy, consisting of the four letters to the Corinthians (1 and 2), Galatians (c. A.D. 55–6) and Romans (c. A.D. 56). The position of the letter to the Galatians will, of course, vary according to our acceptance or rejection of the North Galatian theory, but will not exclude the letter from this second group. Controversy has roused Paul to an intensity of feeling which is reflected in his style of writing, which is now rhetorical, argumentative, forthright, with signs of moral indignation and irony. The Pauline thesis here concerns Christ as Man, Christ as Redeemer, the relation of Law and Faith, Justification, Sanctification, and union with Christ. The Church is His Body.

(3) Thirdly, we have the letters of the first Roman imprisonment (A.D. 58–61) including the letters to the Ephesians, Philippians, and Colossians, together with the personal letter of Philemon, a gentleman of Colosse.[1] The circumstances now draw out a fuller style, heavier, with longer sentences, and very carefully chosen words. It is the language of a philosophical treatise rather than of a polemical pamphlet. Also the circumstances under which these were composed make them the most important documents of the Apostolic Church. Christ's pre-existence in the essential nature of God, His taking upon Himself the essential nature of man, His death and final triumph (*Philippians*); the whole Person of Christ (*Colossians*) and His relation to God, the Universe, and Man; the conception of the one Christian society including in its fold Jew and Gentile alike (*Ephesians*), and representing the ultimate

---

[1] But see my comments on 4 10-11.

purpose of God in the making and governing of the world: all these
were and still are of supreme importance to Christian thought.

(4) Fourthly, we have the letters of the second Roman imprisonment, the so-called Pastoral Epistles to Titus and Timothy
(1 and 2), documents the genuineness of which has been frequently
disputed, and their authenticity in their present form denied, but
which seem to witness in their every expression to the closing
experiences of Paul's life, ranging from about A.D. 62–67. There is
here a marked difference of vocabulary and a simpler mode of
expression, the inevitable result of the changed subject-matter.
But the theology is the same: Christ the Saviour of sinners, the
Mediator between God and man, the Incarnate Christ is now Christ
glorified, the abolition of death and the bringing of life and incor-
ruption to light through the Gospel (1 *Timothy*), and other historical
facts (2 *Timothy*); the Cross as the manifestation of God's eternal
love (*Titus*). Furthermore, the ordinary life of the Church is as
necessary as great theological and philosophical conceptions.
Accordingly here are echoes of the first Group, reminiscences of
the special ideas of the second and third Groups, and directions on
the practical organization and government of Churches.

Reverting to the Third Group. We can easily conceive of the visit
to the imperial city, and of the succeeding months of more or less
enforced leisure as providing the precise circumstances required in
order to call forth the full answer to the question: 'What think ye
of Christ?' Rome had long been the goal of Paul's desire. It is
now the pinnacle from which he sees in clear spiritual vision the
world at the feet of Jesus. At the climax of his career he himself
might well have written what F. W. H. Myers wrote in after-time:

> Then in the midnight, stirring in his slumber,
> Opened his vision on the heights and saw,
> New without name or ordinance or number,
> Set for a marvel, silent for an awe,
> Stars in the firmament above him beaming,
> Stars in the firmament alive and free,
> Stars and of stars the innumerable streaming,
> Deep in the deeps, a river in the sea;
> These as he watched through march of their arising,
> Many in multitude and one by one,
> Somewhat from God with a superb surprising
> Breathed in his eyes the promise of the sun.

It is for this very reason, on the side of Paul's training, we come to our study of his Epistle to the Colossians with the conviction that we are here encountering the ripest teaching of the great master who for twenty arduous years made experience and teaching the two aspects of a witness unique in Christian history, and was now able, at the close of his labours, to give to his word the stamp of an inspired finality. In subject there is no departure from his earliest theme, which is the glory of Christ's Kingdom; but at the end that glory is as the supernal glory of the high noon-day sun as compared with the first rays of the early dawn. His own final word could well be:

> Yea, through life, death, through sorrow and through sinning,
> He shall suffice me, for He hath sufficed:
> Christ is the end, for Christ is the beginning,
> Christ the beginning, for the end is Christ.

It is, however, necessary to view the teaching of the Epistle as the climax to a still more remarkable development than is readily perceived in the training of the Apostle. That training is itself only rightly judged as seen in the light of a larger evolution. Indeed, without this larger perspective we might easily, as some have done, fall into the error of misunderstanding Paul's place in the history of early Christianity. Not a few have been led by an over-concentration on the large part played by the Apostle in the missionary extension of the Church to regard his all-consuming activity as if it involved a departure from the true line of the pure and primitive Christianity of the Gospels which, they affirm, faded away into the tenets of more or less obscure Jewish sects, while this masterful genius, this Aramaic-speaking Greek-thinking Jew of Tarsus, imposed his own conceptions of Christianity upon the Roman world. If this were true, we should have to go elsewhere rather than to the Epistle to the Colossians for an authoritative doctrine of the Christ. Reassurance comes through a careful estimate of the extent to which the Apostle himself is revealed as an instrument prepared, trained, and used for larger purposes than were humanly envisaged. As Napoleon is said to have died confessing in the words 'Head of the army!' a leadership vastly superior to his own, so Paul was ever ready to acknowledge a policy more masterful and infinitely more profound than anything he had either dared to execute or even to conceive. A complete Christology is the work of no apostle, however eminent, and must be studied in the light of something far greater than the outlook of man. No student of the apostolic career should overlook the significance of those strikingly prophetic words in the 49th chapter of Isaiah: 'Hearken, ye people from far: the Lord hath called me from the womb; from the bowels of my mother hath He made mention of my name: and He hath made my mouth like a sharp sword, in the shadow of His hand hath He hid me; and He hath made me a polished shaft, in His quiver hath He kept me close: and He said unto me, Thou art My servant, Israel, in whom I will be glorified.' Could there be a better background for Paul's life? This mighty Apostle put all his will into his work for the Kingdom, but the helm of that will was never in his own hands. Look at a few examples from a cursory survey of his career: he begins, as from his training seemed so fitting, by an attempt to preach to his fellow countrymen, but by circumstances outside his control the attempt is baffled and he is presently led to other circumstances providentially arranged to commence work among the Gentiles. In this he is again and again deflected from his own chosen programme; if he plans to visit Bithynia, his course is changed (probably by illness) towards the highlands of Galatia; if he prays for a robust body in order to give the utmost of his physical powers to a more effective preaching of the Gospel, he is taught by suffering: 'My strength is perfected in weakness'; if he is anxious to conclude a round of visits in Asia Minor, he is summoned by a vision to new work in Europe; if he desires to approach Rome as the untrammelled hero of an all-conquering cause, he is permitted to attain his goal only as a shackled prisoner.

In all this, it is plain that the 'masterfulness' was in the Providence which ruled and directed, but not in the missionary who served the Divine will.

It is for this reason that the Epistle to the Colossians is not merely a personal letter written by one Apostle, but is part of the Bible of the Christian Church; and it is for the same reason that the training of Paul is but a single episode in that vast *preparatio evangelica* which is coincident with all human history. To recognize the evolution of the substance of the Messianic message, without at the same time being thoroughly aware of the remarkable manner in which is also revealed the evolution of its missionary machinery, has been and still is a signal loss to the clarity of our thought of Christianity *as a world fact.* The Old Testament reveals how the world was led on, through animism and henotheism, to the conception of one supreme and universal God. We see also clearly the evolution of morals, of religious institutions, of a religious society, through tribalism and nationalism, to a completer catholicity. We trace the development of the Messianic idea, till the Christ stands before us as the Suffering Servant of Yahweh. Then, when the substance of the message has been declared, we tragically miss perceiving the divine strategy through which the whole field of history is prepared for the proclamation of that message to the world.

Let us, therefore, recall some of the ways in which the Divine direction is revealed in a world to whose doubts and difficulties, disasters and delusions, the doctrine of the Incarnation is intended to be the final answer. Only thus shall we perceive the focal point at which both Paul and his message are placed. First, in the development of the missionary machinery as in that of the Messianic message the Jew had a leading part to play. The painful catastrophe by which Jewish nationalism was shattered and the Dispersion brought about was overruled to provide a world-pulpit for the proclamation of a Gospel that was to be both international and universal. Even the unblushing materialism which drove the Jew from city to city in search of a lucrative commerce was used by God to promote the cause of the spirit, and the very policy which was viewed so suspiciously by the rulers of Jerusalem, by which Judaism became liberalized and centrifugal, created channels along which the stream of Christian thought could the more readily reach the Gentile world. The ubiquity of the Jew at the commencement of the Christian era is a fact of cardinal importance. The Jew was everywhere a force not alone throughout the Roman world; but, beyond that world, considerable Jewish colonies in Babylon and Mesopotamia became another great headquarters of the human race. The Jew became more than the commercial man-of-the-world: he became an eighth part, about a million, of the population of Egypt. In a single massacre at Antioch the Jew yielded up ten thousand of his kind. Add to the ever-increasing number of Jewish people the privilege and influence which brought their witness to the very steps of the throne and the dungeon of the slave, as also to the consciousness of the general population. Wherever ten men of leisure dwelt there was a synagogue in which the Apostles were sure of an interested and often excited audience. Where this was lacking, a *proseuché* (as at Philippi) would be found at the riverside to which resorted whatever Jews were in the vicinity. Of all this far-flung witness of Judaism, Paul was the personal embodiment. All the upsurging passion, the glowing ardour, the untiring zeal, the sheer perdurability of Judaism as the Servant of Jehovah came to a head in his amazing missionary career.

Secondly, there is the extremely important share in the creation of means for propagating the Faith permitted by God to the civilization and language of Greece. It is difficult to think of a more God-controlled career than that of Alexander the Great. To the secular historian everything may seem easy of explanation: Alexander's eastern conquests were but the counter-movement which followed the dismal failure of the grandiose designs of Darius I and Xerxes; indeed his success was predicted by the ease with which Xenophon's soldiers had traversed the hostile satrapies, and the plan of campaign which led to Alexander's passage through Syria into Egypt and the foundation of Alexandria itself was merely to make secure the Macedonian communications by land and sea. What more natural? Yet, as the writer of the book of Daniel describes it, the smiting of the two-horned ram of the Perso-Medic Empire by the mighty horn of the Macedonian he-goat was providentially related to the coming of the Kingdom of the Son of Man. The results, for both East and West, have been remarkable. The wedge of hellenization driven by Alexander into the heart of Asia influenced the Orient as far as China, and Greek speech and culture reigned in Bactria and Parthia long after the Seleucids had passed away. Then, along the pathway cloven to the East, influences came rushing in the reverse direction Westward, such as were to make religious history for centuries to come. East and West were brought face to face, made to speak one another's tongues, and to enter into each other's thought. The creation of a common vernacular for Christendom was as significant as the finding in Judaism of a common pulpit. Imagine what it meant on the day of Pentecost when Jews of the Dispersion, gathered at the great Jerusalem feast, heard the Christian Gospel preached, not in Aramaic or in the Hebrew of the Rabbis, but in the *lingua franca* of the world, the homely Greek. 'We do hear them speak,' they cried, 'in our own tongue the wonderful works of God.' The golden ambitions of Alexander had been overruled and used in order that the vernacular of missionary Christianity might be supplied. Nor was this all; for in this language, since the time of Ptolemy Philadelphus or Ptolemy Philometor, the Jewish scriptures had circulated among the heathen in the form of the Septuagint version (which Paul himself knew well and used freely; a fact which Wendland, for instance, regards as proof that Greek was Paul's 'native tongue'[1]), including the books which, for various reasons, had been excluded from the Hebrew Canon. Indeed we lose much of the significance of the continuous record of revelation in sacred literature if we allow ourselves to forget that the Old Testament for the Christian is not limited by the decision of the Jewish Council of Joppa. The Septuagint, which has not inappropriately been called 'the first apostle to the Gentiles,' is the Old Testament of the Apostles themselves and of the General Councils. It is imperative that we should recognize the singular providence which gave the Greek language its predominance in the world of the Apostles. Moreover, Paul is the embodiment of the witness of hellenization for Christ to the world, although his ideas are better expressed in Hebrew rather than in Greek categories.

Thirdly, we have to recognize also in the Roman world an instrument prepared by the hand of God for the same great end. Unfortunately, our ideas on this matter have been coloured for the most part, first, by the Jewish apocalypses which looked expectantly, eagerly and vindictively, for the total destruction of the blasphemous world-power of Rome which followed the outbreak of the terrible Neronian persecution. Even Paul, in his earliest Epistles, seems inclined to take the strictly Jewish attitude in this respect. But we may too easily forget the immense services rendered by Rome to the extension of the Christian Church during the twenty years of Paul's missionary activity; for it was not merely that he appreciated the facilities of travel on the excellent Roman roads, nor merely that he claimed at various times and occasions the safeguards of his Roman citizenship and received some deferential courtesy at the hands of men like Sergius Paulus and Gallio; but it was more important still for Paul to gather from the extent of the *Pax Romana* and the widespread prestige of Roman organization that vision of a Catholic Christianity which steadily gained strength with the success of his labours: for the material universality of

---

[1] Wendland: *Die hellenistisch-römische Kultur*, p. 354.

Roman dominion was itself a cry for a world religion, and all the efforts to secure religious catholicity by Emperor-worship and later by the hospitality given to cults such as Mithraism were efforts in line with Paul's yearning to win the world for Christ. Indeed the dream of the Holy Roman Empire was not altogether uninspired, nor was Dante altogether wrong in seeing in the founders of the Empire the servants of the Divine idea. Hence, once again, Paul the Jew, born in the cultivated Greek city of Tarsus, Pharisee, Roman citizen, theologian, scholar, traveller, poet, preacher, philosopher, organizer, administrator, brings to a focus all that Rome was inspired to accomplish for the world. Thus, he who was trained in the Rabbinical schools where he received the finest education Judaism could give, and so intensely a Jew that he was willing to be 'accursed' if only he might lead his people to the fulfilment of their true destiny; he who, from his university days at Tarsus, where it is almost inconceivable that he failed to be influenced by Hellenistic thought and Greek philosophy making for a mind compounded of both Hellenistic and Palestinian Judaism, yet always more Jewish than Greek, and wholly Christian, was so deeply sympathetic in his appreciation of Greek culture that he could take a text for a discourse on Areopagus from the pagan classics; he who found so much to admire in the Jurisprudence of Roman Law and the discipline and order of Roman soldiership and administration that he could make his own the proud words *Civis Romanus sum*, is himself prepared of God to interpret the message which had been written over the Cross in letters of Hebrew, Greek, and Latin, the three great languages of the world, 'Jesus of Nazareth, King of the Jews'; lifting up that Cross and its Christ before the eyes of the whole world, concentrating in himself the accumulated passion of mankind to hear and to receive the saving Name, the Name which is above every name, the Name in which the whole vast cosmic order itself would find its necessary redemption. To be adequate for such a task of interpretation was the great purpose of his life's experience, and for this it was given him to grow in the wisdom of a man whose one aim and strategy was planned to convert a world; for this he accepted the sufferings and the sorrows of the toiling years that he might 'fill up' the sorrows and sufferings of his Christ, learning ever more effectually how his weakness might become the channel of a diviner strength; for this he strove to grow in intellectual power and expression that he might tell forth the more convincingly all that God had given him to know. It is this crowning of his message in the Epistle to the Colossians which it is our purpose now to study in close detail.

Paul in bonds at Rome

Let us join Paul in his hired lodgings at Rome, not perhaps in the Jewish quarter where some sixty thousand of his fellow-countrymen resided, but almost certainly in the neighbourhood of the Praetorian Camp, where surveillance over the prisoners awaiting trial might be the more easily exercised. Some time must elapse before Paul could be called up for trial, and the time of waiting, under ordinary circumstances, must have been incredibly tedious. Yet, so keen was his sense of the human, that we can easily imagine his eagerness to use the time as best he could for Christ his Lord; and this he did by writing letters which proved to be of immense importance. Amongst his few pleasures would be the occasional arrival of some fellow-labourer from the Churches of Macedonia, Achaia, or Asia, who, out of devotion to the master, willingly accepted restraint and even became a fellow-prisoner for the time being. In this way he was more than once reminded of the little Christian community at Colosse. First came the evangelist Epaphras with the news, both comforting and disconcerting, of Church conditions in the Lycus valley. Then one day there came, or was brought to him, the runaway slave Onesimus, the property of Paul's Colossian friend Philemon, and then the conversion of the fugitive and the obligation to send him back as speedily as possible to his lawful owner. So it came to pass that when at length another messenger named Tychicus was ready to depart for Asia, Paul was enabled to dispatch three letters: one to Philemon, commending the slave who had now become 'a brother in Christ'; one to the Church of Laodicea, a letter now either lost or known to us under another name; and one most memorable letter to the Church at Colosse, a letter which has become part of the Word of God to all mankind. On arrival, Tychicus is warmly welcomed as the emissary of the Prisoner at Rome. The letter is opened and the list of greetings eagerly scanned.

ANALYSIS OF THE EPISTLE TO THE COLOSSIANS

Section 1. 1 ¹⁻¹⁴

Introduction. Salutation. Thanksgiving for the spiritual progress of the Colossian Christians. Prayer for the enlargement and completion of same.

Section 2. 1 ¹⁵⁻²⁵

The Gospel of the Cosmic Christ: the fundamental doctrinal statement of the Epistle concerning the redeeming Lord and His Kingdom:

(a) His relation to God.
(b) His relation to the Universe.
(c) His Headship of the Church.
(d) The 'fullness' of His Godhead.
(e) Reconciliation in Him.

Section 3. 1 ²⁴⁻²⁹

A parenthesis by way of personal explanation concerning Paul himself and his mission. The revelation of the Mystery.

Section 4. 2 ¹⁻⁷

Paul's present concern for the Colossians and their neighbours.

Section 5. 2 ⁸⁻¹⁵

Paul's polemic against the false Judaeo-Gnostic teaching at Colosse, directed (a) against its general principles as limiting the all-sufficiency of Christ and the Christian's completeness in Him; and—

Section 6. 2 ¹⁶⁻²³

(b) against the religious practices arising from three errors:

(1) Legalism.
(2) Angel-worship.
(3) Asceticism.

Section 7. 3 ¹⁻¹⁷

Paul now proceeds from negative warnings and denunciations to positive injunctions, setting forth with considerable fullness the true Christian life and its practice, as contrasted with the false asceticism and visionary illusions of Theosophy.

Section 8. 3 ¹⁸ 4 ¹

Paul enforces the duties of family life, and (with the case of Onesimus in view) dwells at length on the obligations of husband and wife, father and child, master and servant.

Section 9. 4 ²⁻⁶

Brief exhortations concerning prayer and social conduct.

Section 10. 4 ⁷⁻¹⁷

Paul concludes his Epistle with personal greetings.

Section 11. 4 ¹⁸

The Epistle is sealed by Paul's authenticating signature and final benediction.

CHAPTER I

THE PLENITUDE AND FINALITY OF REDEMPTION

Analysis

Section 1. I [1-14]

    Introduction. Salutation. Thanksgiving for the spiritual progress of the Colossian Christians. Prayer for the enlargement and completion of same.

Section 2. I [15-25]

    The Gospel of the Cosmic Christ: the fundamental doctrinal statement of the Epistle concerning the redeeming Lord and His Kingdom:
    (a) His relation to God.
    (b) His relation to the Universe.
    (c) His Headship of the Church.
    (d) The 'fullness' of His Godhead.
    (e) Reconciliation in Him.

Section 3. I [24-29]

    A parenthesis by way of personal explanation concerning Paul himself and his mission. The revelation of the Mystery.

SECTION I

Authorized Version	*Translation*
THE SALUTATION. I [1-2]	
1 Paul, an apostle of Jesus Christ by the will of God, and Timotheus *our* brother,	1 Paul, an Apostle of Christ Jesus through the will of God, and Timothy our brother,
2 To the saints and faithful brethren in Christ which are at Colosse: Grace *be* unto you, and peace, from God our Father and the Lord Jesus Christ.	2 To those at Colosse who, in Christ, are saints and brethren, and trusty, Grace be to you, and Peace from God our Father.

THE THANKSGIVING FOR SPIRITUAL PROGRESS. I [3-9]

3 We give thanks to God and the Father of our Lord Jesus Christ, praying always for you,

4 Since we heard of your faith in Christ Jesus, and of the love *which ye have* to all the saints,

5 For the hope which is laid up for you in heaven, whereof ye heard before in the word of the truth of the gospel;

6 Which is come unto you, as *it is* in all the world; and bringeth forth fruit, as *it doth* also in you, since the day ye heard *of it*, and knew the grace of God in truth:

7 As ye also learned of Epaphras our dear fellowservant, who is for you a faithful minister of Christ;

8 Who also declared unto us your love in the Spirit.

3 We, (Timothy and I), give thanks to God, Father of our Lord Jesus Christ, praying always for you:

4 having heard (from Epaphras) of your faith in Christ Jesus, and of the love which you have to all the saints,

5 through the hope that is laid up for you in the heavens; of which you have previously heard in the word of Gospel truth:

6 which is present among you, as also in all the world, and is bearing fruit and increasing, as it is amongst you from the day you heard and knew well the grace of God in truth:

7 as you also learned it from Epaphras our beloved fellow-bondman, who is a faithful minister of Christ to you:

8 who likewise has signified to us your love in the Spirit.

A PRAYER FOR COMPLETION IN CHRIST. I [9-14]

9 For this cause we also, since the day we heard *it*, do not cease to pray for you, and to desire that ye might be filled with the knowledge of his will in all wisdom and spiritual understanding;

10 That ye might walk worthy of the Lord unto all pleasing, being fruitful in every good work, and increasing in the knowledge of God;

11 Strengthened with all might, according to his glorious power, unto all patience and longsuffering with joyfulness;

12 Giving thanks unto the Father, which hath made us meet to be partakers of the inheritance of the saints in light:

13 Who hath delivered us from the power of darkness, and hath translated *us* into the kingdom of his dear Son:

9. For this reason we also, from the day we heard these things, do not cease praying for you, asking God that you may be filled with the fuller knowledge of His will in all wisdom and spiritual understanding,

10 in order that you may walk worthy of the Lord to His entire satisfaction, bringing forth fruit by every good work, and increasing in the knowledge of God:

11 In all power being empowered according to the might of His glory, unto all patience and long-suffering with joy,

12 giving thanks to the Father who has made us competent to share in the Light which the Saints inherit:

13 Who has rescued us from the power (dominion) of The Darkness, and has translated us into the Kingdom of His Beloved Son,

14 In whom we have redemption through his blood, *even* the forgiveness of sins:

14 by (in) whom we have redemption through His blood, even the forgiveness of our sins.

Exposition

In order to silence the false teachers who were trying to seduce the Colossian Christians to Judaism, Paul commences the doctrinal part of his Letter with confuting their leading error, namely, that the institutions of Moses and especially the Levitical sacrifices were still necessary, because there were no propitiatory sacrifices in the Gospel. This false and destructive doctrine the Apostle repudiates by showing that they who are 'translated into the kingdom of God's Beloved Son have redemption through *His* blood, even the forgiveness of sins,' and consequently that in the Gospel dispensation God Himself has appointed a redemption of complete and final efficacy to which every believer can turn for pardon, without the need of any other propitiatory sacrifice whatsoever, Levitical or otherwise.

This claim needs careful consideration at the outset of our study in preparation for the complete understanding of Paul's central theme, namely, the Supreme Lordship of Christ; of Christ as King of all the Universe, of all worlds visible and invisible; of all powers, political, sociological, scientific, ethical, philosophical, natural, economic, theological; in short, the historic Christ seen in universal setting as the Cosmic Christ, such being His nature and significance. The redemption of mankind is bound up with the universe itself, since redemption, to be effective and efficient, must be wholly and absolutely *universal*.

Let us, therefore, look closely at verse 14.

> *By (or, in) whom we have redemption through His blood, even the forgiveness of our sins.*
> (cf. *Eph.* 1 [7]; *Gal.* 3 [10-13]; *Rom.* 3 [19-26]; 5 [9]; 2 *Cor.* 5 [18-21]; 1 *Pet.* 3 [18-19].)

Redemption—ἀπολύτρωσις, lit. 'a buying back, or the giving of something in exchange.' This powerful word is full of spiritual meaning, a word for awakening the intuition rather than a theological technicality aiming at exact definition. It suggests the idea of 'purchase' or 'acquisition by sacrifice.'—'Ye were sealed into the redemption of the thing acquired' (*Eph.* 1 [11]). 'Ye are not your

D

own, ye were bought with a price.' But the seller is not the Devil, as early Patristic theology claimed; neither is the transaction one between Infinite Mercy and Infinite Justice. The true ἀπολύτρωσις touches the inner springs of being; it is not an external adjustment of relations between a man's soul and a God outside him; it is rather the process by which a man is won to the realization of a mislaid and forgotten sonship. Redemption becomes a dogma by virtue of its being an essential spiritual experience. It is the foundation and substance of the mystic life projected by the intellect into form and dogma on the external plane; for what the soul experiences, the intellect formulates. Thus the *apolutrōsis*, which is one of the deepest truths of the spiritual life, may be expressed only tentatively in terms of a human transaction. It is an eternal process of substitution by which a man reverses the entire scheme of human values, and makes prominent in consciousness what had been hitherto but a dim background in his unfelt, spiritual, being. By its operation the laws of 'the Spirit which is life' supplant the legalism whose source is 'the old Adam.' The truly *redeemed man* is he who has tasted at least the beginning of the great Restoration; he stands where he can feel again the stirrings of that Divine consciousness which he knew before he had broken unity with God and eaten of the fruit of self and separation. He has set out to regain the spiritual life, but at a cost which is terribly hard to pay.

How then can the physical life of Jesus, outpoured on Calvary's Cross, avail to effect what must ever be personal, interior, deeply rooted in the individual will? The answer perhaps lies this way—Christ's crucifixion was an event in Time that was a symbol of a fact that is Eternal. The very existence of the symbol as an outward and visible sign of a universal, hidden, and eternal Power ceaselessly poured forth in exchange for the ills and weaknesses of men, puts those who make use of it in conscious touch with the Reality whose expression in a very particular sense it is. 'We are conformed to the image of His death,' argues Paul, as if to affirm that by a symbol, or outer representation, we are united to that great Death of which the Calvary event is the 'image' or picturing-forth in time-relations, and to which the disciple must shape himself in heart if he would know the life that is 'life indeed;' in short, the life given in exchange is the sign-manual of the perfected Christ. Such an One is living, both symbolically and actually, the life of the race within 'the form of a servant,' which He assumes as a touch-point with humanity, a centre whence the Divine Spirit may flow forth in blessing, and into which may be received all the poisonous evils of the sinful nature He comes to 'take away.'

Thus the Pauline affirmation that 'He was made (became) sin . . . that we might become the Righteousness of God in Him' is a statement of the principle of *apolutrōsis*, or exchange, which is not only consistent with the laws of the spiritual life, but is the actual condition of there being a spiritual life at all. Christ offers the highest in exchange for the lowest, and, by associating Himself with the sin-state, associates also the sin-state with Himself, so 'putting it away.' He takes away sin by the 'giving forth' of Himself. In Him the New Man had come to complete possession.

Through His blood. To Paul, Christ was, without a shadow of uncertainty, the great Revealer of the Spiritual Man. Therefore the saying: 'In whom we have redemption through His blood, even the putting away of sins,' was Paul's symbolic form of stating the great law of the Spiritual Man, namely, that the outpouring of the Perfect Life upon conditions of sin and disharmony and disease restores the wholeness that once was theirs, as a highly skilled physician or surgeon or psychiatrist 'redeems' or 'buys back' to health, often at something considerably more than the cost of his hard-won knowledge, the bodies and minds in which some physical or mental ill is at work. In the case of Christ, the expression of this truth holds good even to every outward detail of the physical plane, so much so that the manner of His death has a significance that is wholly Cosmic. 'The blood of Calvary' is a transcription of the world-pages of 'Christ' in terms of suffering, renunciation, sacrificial love, redemption, and final triumph. Christ being Cosmic, the Perfect Man in whom heaven and earth meet, and the representative of the future corporate consciousness of the race, in Him all things and all human wills were potentially offered, not as an act of appeasement to an 'angry god' but as a condition of union with God who so loved the world that He gave His all to restore it to His Heart.

I am, of course, well aware that such interpretation will not satisfy those who seek a definitely *Theological* explanation of Paul's meaning here, and none other. Let us therefore turn to that aspect of the problem.

Dr. Vincent Taylor, in two scholarly works, *Jesus and His Sacrifice* (1939) and *The Atonement in New Testament Teaching* (1946), has some highly significant comments on this subject. In the former work he says: 'More and more students of comparative religion . . . are insisting that the bestowal of life is the fundamental idea in sacrificial worship. The victim is slain in order that its life, in the form of blood, may be released. . . . The aim is to make it possible for life to be presented as an offering to the Deity' (pp. 54 f.). And in the latter work he says: The term blood 'suggests the thought of life, dedicated, offered, transformed, and opened to our spiritual appropriation' (p. 198). Thus, according to Dr. Taylor, being redeemed by the 'blood' of Jesus means being redeemed by His 'life.' If this is so, does the *death* of Jesus cease to have the centrality and the efficacy which the Church has universally attributed to it? Must His *death* be reckoned as merely incidental?

On the contrary, Dr. Leon Morris has pointed out in his book, *The Apostolic Preaching of the Cross* (1955), that the evidence afforded by the term 'blood' as used in the Old Testament signifies 'life violently taken' rather than the continued presence of life available for new functions. Similarly Stibbs in *The Meaning of the word 'Blood' in Scripture* (1947) suggests that 'Blood shed stands not for the release of life from the burden of the flesh, but for the bringing to an end of life in the flesh. It is a witness to physical death, not an evidence of spiritual survival.' In the New Testament, it is important to observe that the largest group of passages containing the word 'blood' refers to violent death (cf. *Acts* 22 [20]; *Rev.* 6 [10]); and there are many references to the 'blood of Jesus' which show that death and not life is obviously meant. A few examples will suffice: (i) Rom. 5 [9]: 'justified by His blood,' 'saved from the wrath through Him.' The conclusion that 'His blood' refers to the *death* of Christ seems irrefutable. (ii) Heb. 9 [14f]: 'How much more shall the blood of Christ . . . cleanse your conscience from dead works to serve the living God? And for this cause He is the mediator of the New Testament, that by means of *death having taken place*. . . .' (iii) Heb. 12 [24]: we read of coming to 'Jesus the mediator of a new covenant, and to the blood of sprinkling that speaketh better things than that of Abel.' Here the blood of Jesus is sharply contrasted with that of Abel, both pointing to death. (iv) Heb.

13 [11f]: Here we observe the comparison made between the sin-offering and the blood of Jesus, the point being not the presentation of the blood shed, but the burning of the carcase outside the camp. The emphasis is laid on the death of the animal, not the presentation of life. The sacrificial illustration points straight to the death of Christ, whose life is given up in death in all its redemptive meaning, 'that we might be made the righteousness in Him by whom we have the forgiveness of our sins' (*Col.* I [14, 21, 22]; 2 [13,14]; 2 [13]; 2 *Cor.* 5 [21]; *Rom.* 4 [25]; 5 [1]; 8 [1]; *Titus* 2 [14]; *Heb.* 9 [14]; 10 [1-18]; I *Pet.* 2 [24]; I *John* I [7]–2 [2]; 4 [10]). (v) Rom. 3 [24] gives its objective ground. The 'redemption of the body,' also 'bought' by the same 'price' (I *Cor.* 6 [20]) will make the work complete (*Eph.* I [13, 14]; *Rom.* 8 [19-23]; I *Cor.* I [30]).

Bp. Lightfoot suggests that the Apostle here intends to contradict the doctrine of Redemption taught by the Gnostics who made it consist in initiation into their 'mysteries'; and supposes that this idea was already in existence at Colosse in some incipient form. But such an abuse of the term appears to imply a well-established and familiar Christian use. Philo, however, who speaks the language of the Jewish philosophic mysticism of the first century, has no such usage.

For St. Paul, this at least is clear: 'redemption through His blood' was the triumphant certainty of 'the forgiveness of our sins.' Formerly 'at enmity with God' because of sinfulness, Christ had now 'made peace.' This was the certainty which Paul proclaimed everywhere. Christians had the proof of it within themselves. They knew what deliverance from sin meant: something that had been done in them and for them. Christ alone had done it. Christ alone had brought them life. Paul was not, like so many apologists of our modern age, content to offer what we may be ready to regard as an *improved ideology*. That may be thought urgent enough, but it is not the Gospel of Redemption. Our modern danger lies in holding to all the 'assurances' which human nature seeks to live by instead of the wholly Christian assurance of salvation which only Christ provides. Faith in the comfortable props of a Welfare State is by no means the same as being saved from the sins of a luxury-loving people; indeed the man who tries to add Christ's assurance to his own bundle of self-assurance forfeits everything. So, too, the Church which would play safe with worldly security and guide itself mainly by the predictable certainties of human wisdom loses in the end the Christian certainty which it is supposed to be preaching.

A Summary of 1 ⁹⁻¹⁴, *and a Study of the outstanding features of Paul's prayer.*

Paul's opening prayer rises out of his previous thanksgiving, and leads up to the chief doctrinal statement of the Epistle (verses 15–20). The immediate concern of Paul's prayer, as in other letters of this period, is the Church's need of spiritual knowledge (cf. *Eph.* 1 ¹⁷⁻¹⁸; *Phil.* 1 ⁹⁻¹⁰). Here this desire finds its fullest expression, since the Colossians' need in this respect was the more urgent and their situation the more fully representative of the stage in the history of the Pauline Churches now commencing. Accordingly he asks his readers (i) to ensure for themselves a fuller knowledge of the Divine will (verse 9), which is to result in (ii) greater God-pleasing (verse 10a) due to (iii) increased moral fruitfulness and spiritual growth (verse 10b), to (iv) patience under suffering (verse 11) and to (v) thankfulness for the blessings of redemption (verses 12–14).

Of the outstanding features of Paul's prayer observe—

1. *The first and most remarkable fact is the use made by Paul of the Gnostic terminology*, a use which some scholars have urged as a ground for rejecting the genuineness of the Epistle, but which is entirely natural if we think of the writer as anxious to display the full scope of the Christian faith. He will not stand upon the use or disuse of mere terms. He seems to say—Very well, if you are not content with *my* terms, I am ready to use *yours*, and to show that the Christ answers all you seek, whether under one set of terms or under another. I am therefore willing to *de-polarize* (so to speak) my terms in the interest of a common understanding and common acceptance. (Paul might profitably have added: And I commend this method to the future theologians of the Church who may cling too tenaciously to the language of their theological schools!) This is how I, at least, understand Paul's use, at the very commencement of this Epistle, even in his prayer to God, of terms like *Pleroma* (fullness), *Epignosis* (full knowledge), *Sophia* (wisdom), and *Synesis* (under-

THE PLENITUDE AND FINALITY OF REDEMPTION

standing). The misuse of these terms in the interests of heresy must
not be allowed to preclude their use in the interest of truth.

2. It is in line with this use of terms that Paul reveals from the outset
that *Orthodoxy is not limiting, cramping, or confining, but is the Christian
claim to enjoy in both belief and experience the maximum rather than the
minimum*. If this were always duly accepted, we should be spared
the spectacle of disgruntled people leaving a supposedly 'narrow'
communion for something 'broad' and 'liberal.' What indeed
could be more liberal than this earnest prayer that men may be
filled? Or what intellectual goal could be set higher than the *full
knowledge* of God's will? Or what conception of life could be richer
than that which asks of God *every kind of wisdom and understanding*?
Christians may fail by asking too little, but never by expecting too
much.

3. *The prayer maps out the proper development of the Christian life,
leading to triumphant achievement*. (i) There is, first, its source in 'the
full knowledge' of God's will. (ii) Then its course in 'the worthy,
daily walk.' (iii) Finally its fourfold result: (a) fruitfulness in good
works, (b) increase in the knowledge of God's will, (c) strengthening
unto patience and longsuffering. and (d) as the climax, the attitude
of thanksgiving which transforms life into an abiding Eucharist.

Just as in the Church Catechism the privileges which are assured
by God are set forth before our own responsibilities are recited,
so here in this Epistle, Paul is careful to insist that the Christian life
must be built upon the solid reality of what God has already effected.
It is not for men, by painful scrupulosities of asceticism, to strain
and struggle up by some tortuously steep ascent to God; it is rather
theirs to recognize with the humbleness of a thankful heart that God
has already in Christ broken through every intervening barrier
and won the Eternal Victory over all the powers of darkness.

Antiochus had brought away only some two thousand reluctant
families to dwell within the valley of the Lycus, but God has
ransomed all humanity from the kingdom of darkness and the
powers of evil, as He has, by holy baptism, translated His redeemed
children into the kingdom of the Son of His eternal love. Slaves
already redeemed do not have again to redeem themselves. Here
and now, in the enriching experience of the Christian life, men are
face to face with the privileges and the responsibilities of the new
citizenship. Christ-redeemed people are 'meet to be partakers,'

not in the sense of being 'fit,' but as *made competent* (verse 12: so the Greek ἱκανώσαντι implies) to use their inheritance. They are all members of Christ, children of God, and inheritors of the kingdom of heaven. This is the true starting-point. 'Full right' belongs to every Christian.

> Thou hast it; use it, and forthwith, or die!
> For I say, this is death, and the sole death,
> When a man's loss comes to him through his gain,
> Darkness from light, from knowledge ignorance,
> And lack of love from love made manifest.

Such is Paul's introduction to his great theme. So the way is now clear for the setting forth of the Christ as in very truth accomplishing for the world and for men all that the human heart had yearned and striven for, but, apparently, in vain.

SECTION 2. THE PAULINE THESIS OF THE COSMIC CHRIST

Authorized Version   *Translation*

CHRIST'S RELATION TO GOD. I 15

15 Who is the image of the invisible God, the firstborn of every creature:

15 Christ is the perfect image of God the invisible, the Father's first-born and Prince of the whole Creation.

CHRIST'S RELATION TO THE UNIVERSE. I 16-17

16 For by him were all things created, that are in heaven, and that are in earth, visible and invisible, whether *they be* thrones, or dominions, or principalities, or powers: all things were created by him, and for him:

17 And he is before all things, and by him all things consist.

16. For in Him were created all things in the heavens and on the earth, the things visible and the things invisible, whether Thrones, or Lordships, or Principalities, or Dominions. All things through Him and unto Him have been created:

17 He existed before everything, and in Him everything consists (coheres, constitutes a single whole).

CHRIST'S RELATION TO THE CHURCH. I 18

18 And he is the head of the body, the church: who is the beginning, the firstborn from the dead; that in all *things* he might have the preeminence.

18 He is also the Head of the Divine Body, the Church. He is the beginning, the first-born out of the dead, that in all things He might be pre-eminent.

The Fullness of Christ's Godhead. 1 [19]

19 For it pleased *the Father* that in him should all fulness dwell;

19 For it pleased the Father that in Him the Fullness (plenitude of Deity) should dwell, without limit.

Reconciliation of All in Christ. 1 [20-23]

20 And, having made peace through the blood of his cross, by him to reconcile all things unto himself; by him, *I say*, whether *they be* things in earth, or things in heaven.

21 And you, that were sometime alienated and enemies in *your* mind by wicked works, yet now hath he reconciled

22 In the body of his flesh through death, to present you holy and unblameable and unreproveable in his sight:

23 If ye continue in the faith grounded and settled, and *be* not moved away from the hope of the gospel, which ye have heard, *and* which was preached to every creature which is under heaven; whereof I Paul am made a minister;

20 And was also pleased by Him to reconcile all things to Himself, having made peace by the blood of His cross: I repeat, by Him, whether they are things upon the earth, or things in the heavens:

21 Even you, who were formerly alienated in mind, and enemies by your actively evil works, God has now reconciled—

22 through His physical death, to present you holy and blameless and faultless in His sight—

23 if only you continue in the faith, founded and stable, and not moved away (earthquake stricken) from the hope of the Gospel which you have heard, which has been proclaimed to every creature under heaven, and of which I, Paul, am made a minister.

Exposition

The significance of Paul's thesis that Christ is 'the image of the invisible God, the first-born of all creation, by whom all things were created in the heavens and on the earth, things visible and things invisible, whether thrones or dominions or principalities or powers; everything has been created through Him and unto Him, and He is before all things, and in Him all things consist'—in short, that Christ is the *Cosmic Christ*, cannot be exaggerated. It is the intellectual miracle of the Apostolic age. Only thirty years had passed since Jesus of Nazareth was 'crucified under Pontius Pilate'; and yet here in his Letter to the Colossians is the converted Saul of Tarsus, by a daring leap of the imagination, declaring that this same Jesus was God's agent in the creation of the universe, that He is the sustaining power that maintains its life, and the ultimate goal to which it is working its way, the centre of the divine event to which the whole creation moves.

Allowing for all the necessary categories and theological formulae that were already to hand in the storehouse of Jewish, Greek, and Oriental cults of the time, the question which the serious scholar must solve is: Why was Jesus of Nazareth, and He alone, chosen to bear the highest honour and dignity ever placed upon a human brow? The solution of this problem must be looked for in Paul's personal religious experience. The resurrection of Jesus was the supreme fact for Paul. The living, ascended, reigning Christ was an abiding spiritual presence in his life. The post-existence of Jesus implied His pre-existence also, and this had, for Paul, as much validity as the inverse argument of Plato in the *Phaedo* for the immortality of the soul. If therefore the pre-existence of Jesus is a valid thesis, Paul cannot but pass to the investigation of the character of His activity in His pre-existent state. It is here that Paul makes the most daring intellectual claim known to the history of thought. Christ had already become the centre of Paul's moral universe, and from that comes the inevitable conclusion that He must always have been the centre of the life of the universe as a whole.

Is this a valid deduction? Is it legitimate to argue from the moral to the cosmic sphere? Unless we are prepared to acquiesce in a final metaphysical dualism, the answer is that in the ultimate issue moral reality and cosmic reality must originate in the same source and be two aspects of the same final fact.

Thus the Colossian thesis represents the real creative moment in the history of Christology. When once this position was reached, the Prologue to the Fourth Gospel and the historic creeds of Christendom followed logically. These are simply the interpretations and elucidations, in more philosophical phraseology, of the Colossian thesis: Jesus is the Cosmic Christ, a heavenly pre-existent Divine Being who was God's agent in the creation of the universe, over which He is Lord of all. Thus it is one of the great achievements of the Pauline mind that, out of his personal experience of the Living Christ, he evolved a philosophy of the Christian religion which has been the centre of orthodox Christian doctrine ever since, and which is being constantly verified in Christian experience to this day.

Paul had in view theosophic theories of the universe which were exercising a pernicious fascination on the minds of some Christians, as indeed they still do, and which, while they seemed to bring 'principalities and powers' into captivity to Christ, were really reducing Him from the peerless platform which was His own, to their level. But Paul would have nothing so nebulous; he saw in Christ a pre-existent Being who was both creator and upholder of the universe, who appeared on earth as redeemer and emancipator through whom a reconstituted creation would attain, at length, its grand ideal.

Here Paul's conception of Christ reaches its sublimest expression. Christ stands alone in absolute eminence where none can compete with Him. He is 'the image of the invisible God' in whom, as a cosmological basis, 'all things consist.'

Paul was well aware that Jesus was a real man, but he was very sure that God had dwelt and wrought in Him and through Him, in a wholly unique manner shared by none other. He was God manifest in the flesh; reason, mind, and love of God revealed and interpreted in terms of human life and experience.

The question at once arose: how were Paul and other Christian thinkers to express their sense of the real significance of Christ? They found the answer, first, by searching the vocabulary of their age for essential terms in which to give adequate expression to their belief. Consequently they called Him the 'image' or 'impress' of God; the 'first-born' or 'only begotten Son of God'; the 'outshining of the Divine Majesty'; the 'Word' or 'self-expression'; the 'uttered reason of God'; the 'eternal wisdom of God' through whose co-operation 'God formed the worlds' (see *Col.* 1 [15]; *Heb.* 1 [3]; *John* 1 [18]; *Heb.* 1 [2]; *John* 1 [1,14]; 1 *Cor.* 1 [24]; *Col.* 1 [16]; *John* 1 [3]). By such terms as these, which were current coin of the Jewish and Alexandrian thought-worlds of the period, did Paul and others express the results of the experiences and reflections concerning Jesus. In some profound and mysterious sense the roots of His being were in God. He was the Divine-Human Personality, the interpreter of God to man, and of man to himself. In Him the nature, will and world-purpose of God was fully revealed in human terms. He was the 'truth' of God's being, the self-expression and translation of God in, and into, terms of our humanity. Thus in the mystery of His person were the 'hidden treasures' (*Col.* 2 [3]) which were not accessible to mere reason or intellect, but only to spiritual apprehension.

But more than this, in Christ Paul sees God's 'coefficient' in the creation and administration of the world. His work is the realization of God's eternal world-plan (*Col.* 1 [15-18]; *Eph.* 3 [9-11]). Christ is not merely the historic person whom we call by that name, but the 'principle' (ἀρχή) of the creation (*Col.* 1 [15-18]) and the medium of a universal reconciliation (*Col.* 1 [19, 20]). Thus, verses 15–23 constitute a most remarkable thesis, and this section alone occupies a place in the Christology of St. Paul which corresponds to that contained in Romans 3 [19-26] which treats of his Soteriology. Here in these verses he treats expressly of the Universal and Cosmic sovereignty of Christ and the true nature of His person; subjects which elsewhere in his writings are for the most part matter of assumption or mere incidental reference. But the paragraph is not detached or regarded as an isolated piece of abstract theology or speculative philosophy. It depends both grammatically and practically on the three previous verses (12, 13, 14). It sets forth who Christ is and the place He fills in the universe: He is that Son of God's love in whom we have redemption, and in whose Kingdom the Father has placed us; and what cause, therefore, there is for the Colossian Christians, as indeed for all, to give thanks as having such a person for their redeeming King.

Thus, lest the Colossians might have fallen under the influence of Judaizing critics who argued that the pardon of the sins of the whole world was an effect too great to be ascribed to one man's shedding of blood, Paul observes that the atonement made by that one sacrifice is absolute, since it was *Christ's* blood that was shed, and therefore perfectly sufficient for the redemption of sin. It was the supreme Sovereignty of Christ which enhanced the merit of His death. This supreme dignity Paul described in a magnificence of language required by the grandeur of the subject. Christ is the incarnation of God and Lord of the whole creation, for whom was created 'all things in heaven and earth, visible and invisible,' and by whom all things are upheld since in Him all things find coherence. Having thus described the original dignity of Christ as God's beloved Son, for the purpose of displaying the merit of His death, Paul proceeds to speak of the honour and power which He received, in the human nature, as the reward of His death, thereby showing the folly of those who endeavoured to persuade the Colossians to prefer the mediation of angels to that of Christ. He is the head of all things, and of the Church, indeed the very foundation of it all, since He it was who originated it. Moreover, He is also the 'Lord of the dead,' having Himself died to raise them again to life. This greatness, both in the natural and the spiritual spheres, He has received from the Father, that He may unite angels and men in one great community under Himself as their head, in happy subjection to God and in the society of the Redeemed, to all eternity. For it pleased the Father that in Jesus Christ all the fullness of perfection and power should for ever abide, and through the exercise of His authority and power, by Him to unite all things to Himself as head, having 'made peace' between them by the 'blood of His Cross,' thus closing the gap between Himself and us, between Himself and the world, between our guilt and His own perfect offering to the Almighty Father. Even the idolatrous Gentiles, despite their former wickedness, He has thus united in one body with the Jews, in His Church, through the death on Calvary, to redeem them spotless and blameless in Christ's sight at the final day. To be thus presented before Christ, Paul urged the Colossians to believe would be their happy lot, since they were continuing firm in the faith of the Gospel-doctrine which, because of its efficacy to save and sanctify sinners, was preached to every creature under heaven; of which Gospel Paul received his commission as a minister direct from Christ Himself.

Considered more fully, this short passage which consists of only six verses falls into two parts, closely corresponding both in form and sense, and governed, like other Pauline utterances, by a Hebraistic antithetical rhythm of expression which, rightly understood, makes easier the difficulties of its interpretation. A twofold headship is ascribed to the Lord Christ—

(1) Natural—verses 15–17,
(2) Redemptional—verses 18–20,

the first being the source and ground of the second; the second being the issue of the first, its reassertion and consummation.

Analysis

(1) *Natural*—verses 15–17.

15. (a) who is the Image of God the invisible, Firstborn of all creation:

16. (b) For in Him were created all things
    (c) in the heavens and on the earth the things visible and
        the things invisible, whether Thrones, Lordships,
        Principalities, Dominions:
17. (d) All things through Him and for Him have been created:
    (e) and He is prior to all things, and in Him all things have
        their consistency and coherence.

(2) *Redemptional*—verses 18–20.

18. (e) And He is the Head of the Body, the Church:
    (a) Who is the Beginning, Firstborn out of the dead, that
        in all things He might be pre-eminent:
19. (b) For in Him, He was pleased that all the fullness should
        dwell without limit:
20. (d) and in His Person to reconcile everything, having made
        peace through the blood of His Cross;
    (e) whether the things on earth or the things in the heavens.

Accordingly

(1) (a) in virtue of His relation to God, Christ is
    (b) ground of creation
    (c) both in heaven and earth; and at the same time
    (d) its means and end. He is, therefore,
    (e) supreme over the universe, pre-conditioning its existence,
        and constituting its unity.
(2) In a similar sense He is
    (e) Head of the Church,
    (a) in virtue of His new relation to man, which makes Him
    (b) ground,
    (d) means, and end of reconciliation also,
    (c) both in earth and in heaven; i.e. the whole universe.

Looked at in detail we have the following:

(a) CHRIST'S RELATION TO GOD, I [15].

'Who is the image of God the invisible, the Father's firstborn,
and Prince of the whole Creation.'

If Christ is, in truth, the Divine Ideal of Man, then it follows
that He is also that Ideal for *all* mankind. This is no mere assertion
of a metaphysical idea concerning His person. It has a sober,

practical bearing. It concerns His relation to the universe as well as to God. In relation to God, He is 'the Son of His love.' He is 'the image of God.' He participates in the Deity, in human form. But He, as 'Son,' is clearly distinguished from God as 'Father.' It is God-the-Father who does everything in and through God-the-Son. As the 'firstborn of all Creation' He is 'before all things,' not merely a product of them, and all things were created *in* Him as their Ideal, *through* Him as instrumental cause, and *unto* Him as final cause. Thus, 'in Him' the whole universe 'consists,' holds together as a definite consistent whole, a Cosmos.

Thus Paul goes beyond the value of Christ for personal salvation. He affirms the cosmic significance of Christ. The fact is that the *finality* of Christ was being challenged. Man was said to be in the grip of cosmic-forms and spirit-agencies with which Christ had no ability to cope. Man was left helpless in a terrifying world from which there seemed to be no escape. Paul answered the challenge by affirming the absoluteness of Christ. Paul had already conferred on Christ the title 'the visible image of God' in 2 Cor. 4 [4], in which the moral and redemptional attributes of the Godhead are manifested in the 'illumination of the Gospel' that Jesus is the incarnate Redeemer. Here, however, the title is given Him as representing the invisible God in all that pertains to nature and creation. Christ is called now, in addition, 'the express image of His substance' (*Heb.* 1 [3]), because in the creation of all things He exhibited the perfections peculiar to God (cf. *Rom.* 1 [20]). Generally the word 'image' denotes likeness, sameness of nature and properties. Like the image of Caesar on the coin brought to Jesus by the Pharisees, the revelation of Christ brings home to men the Supreme Ruler of the universe in His perfect likeness, His full representativeness, and in the completeness of His manifestation. Or, to use a simpler illustration, just as in Norwich Cathedral mirrors mounted on trolleys which can be moved along the floors of nave and cloister enable the visitor to study in detail the exquisite bosses on the ceilings, so the revelation of Christ makes it possible for man to see what would otherwise be beyond all human vision.

No religion may tolerate a deism in which God is eternally remote from men. A wholly transcendental God can never satisfy the human need of a divine companion. Although the saintly Rabindranath Tagore's *King of the Dark Chamber* emphasizes in beautiful form the Christian truth: 'Blessed are they who have not seen, and yet have believed,' nevertheless there is a profound difference between the 'gracious twilights where God's chosen lie' and the 'thick darkness' in which He is supposed to dwell for ever hid. The Indian poet's Unitarianism tells but half the truth, and Queen Sudarshana may well crave for a more human fellowship than her lord vouchsafes, if she is to be saved from the 'trumped-up Kings.' Nevertheless it is plain that no ray of Godhead, unmediated by compassion for human frailties, may reach the mind of man without ruin and blasting. The Talmudic story relates that, had the prayer of Moses that he might see God face to face been granted, one spark of the Divine presence must have scorched him to a cinder. As the poet puts it:

> Pure faith indeed—you know not what you ask!
> Naked belief in God the Omnipotent,
> Omniscient, Omnipresent, sears too much
> The sense of conscious creatures to be borne.
> It were the seeing Him no flesh shall dare,
> Under the vertical sun the exposed brain,
> And lidless eye and disemprisoned heart
> Less certainly would wither up at once
> Than mind, confronted with the truth of Him.

Nor, again, is the void between God and man to be bridged satisfactorily by any chain of beings 'half abstractions and half persons,' such as may link together the material and the spiritual. Men crave touch with no *Demiurgus*, no journeyman God, taking up our human problems with apprentice hand. They are not content, with the rebels of Israel, to appeal to some human mediator such as Moses: 'Speak *thou* to us and we will hear: let not *the Lord* speak to us lest we die.' Rather, with the author of the *Imitatio* will they the more assuredly pray: 'Not thus, O Lord, not thus do I pray; but rather with Samuel the prophet I humbly and longingly entreat Thee: speak, Lord, for Thy servant heareth.' All this the Christ makes possible, for He makes God present and visible. He fills the universe from depth to height with God, and makes the human soul His Holy of Holies. All the half-gods go when He appears. Even Moses and Elias fade from sight, and Jesus is 'left alone.'

The Colossian error which Paul is seeking to correct rested on a philosophical dualism: it assumed an absolute separation between the infinite God and the finite material world which was regarded as the work of a lower, inferior, and more or less evil power. Thus, in order to counteract the heresy, Paul's argument must necessarily go down to the very foundation of things, and establish a true conception of the universe on which to base itself. Accordingly in this and the verses following, he bases the redeeming work of 'the Word made flesh who dwelt among us,' set forth in his previous Epistles, upon that of 'the Word who was with God in the beginning, who was God, and through whom all things were made.' He avoids, however, the term *Logos*, which must have been perfectly familiar to him in this connection, possibly to prevent misunderstanding. But this brings him to the consideration of Christ's relation to Nature, namely—*The firstborn and Prince of the whole creation* (cf. *Rom.* 8 [19, 22, 29]; *Heb.* 1 [2, 6]; *John* 1 [18]; *Ps.* 89 [27])—*firstborn*—prior in time to all created works. He is outside of creation, and is the link between the created world and the self-existent God. The universe has no terrors for a man who belongs to Christ. It is perhaps impossible, certainly difficult, to understand rightly the meaning here without accurate knowledge of primogeniture.

(i) In early times primogeniture carried with it the rights of full heirship, which also involved representation of the father in both his civil and religious capacity, as well as in his sovereignty within the home (see *Gen.* 25 [31]; 27 [29]; 49 [3]; *Deut.* 21 [17]; 1 *Chron.* 5 [1]; 2 *Chron.* 21 [3]). Hence among the Hebrews and other ancient nations, firstborn, heir, and lord were synonymous terms (cf. *Gal.* 4 [1]: 'As long as the heir is a child, he is nothing different from a bond-man, though he be lord of all'). *Heres apud antiquos pro Domino ponebatur* (cf. Justinian: *Institutes*, lib. 2, tit. 19).

(ii) But natural precedence, as in the case of Esau and Jacob (*Gen.* 27 [37]) may yield to divine election, which gives a unique sacredness and separateness to the position and title of the firstborn. So Israel is Yahweh's firstborn among the nations (*Exod.* 4 [22-23]; *Jer.* 31 [9]).

(iii) What belonged to the Chosen People under this title is, in the language of Psalm 89 [27], concentrated on the person of the Messianic King, the elect son of David: thus *firstborn* became a standing designation of the Messiah.

(iv) St. Paul has already applied it to Christ in His relation to the

E

Church (*Rom.* 8 [29]) as being not 'the eldest' simply, but one intrinsically superior to and sovereign over those whom He claims for His brethren (cf. *Rom.* 14 [9]). Here the historical birthright and actual sovereignty of the Lord Jesus within the Church are affirmed to rest upon an *original primacy over the universe itself.* He is not the Church's only, but 'all creation's Firstborn' (cf. *Heb.* 3 [3-6]: 'Son over his own house'—the house of him 'who built all things'). The phrase is synonymous with the 'Heir of all things' of Hebrew 1 [2], and the 'Only-begotten' of John 1 [18].

(v) So far were the titles 'Firstborn' and 'Only-begotten' from excluding each other in Jewish thought that Israel is designated 'God's firstborn, only-begotten,' in the apocryphal Psalms of Solomon (18 [4]; also 2 Esdras 6 [58]); and so completely had the former become a title of sovereignty that God Himself is called 'Firstborn of the World' by Rabbi Bechai.

(vi) Philo uses the equivalent πρωτόγονος of the Divine Word as the seat of the archetypal ideas after which creation was framed.

(vii) This phrase has been a famous battleground of controversy. It was a chief stronghold of the Arians according to whom the firstborn of the whole creation is 'the first made creature.' But the Son's creating all things does not prove Him to be the first made creature, unless indeed His power of creating all things originated from His being the first-made creature, which no one, surely, will affirm. As little does the Son's creating all things prove that He first of all created Himself. Thus the Arians read 'of (or, out of) all creation' as partitive genitive. While grammatically permissible, this interpretation is exegetically and historically impossible; for verses 16–17 emphatically distinguish between 'him' and the 'all things' of creation. The idea of the Son of God being *part of* creation was entirely foreign to Paul's mind (see 2 [9]; 1 *Cor.* 8 [6]; *Phil.* 2 [6-8]), and also to the thought of his day. Had such a misunderstanding occurred to him as possible, he would doubtless have expressed himself differently.

It is to be observed that Paul does not call our Lord πρωτοκτιστον πάσης κτίσεως, 'the first created of all creatures,' but πρωτότοκος πάσης κτίσεως, 'the firstborn of every creature, the first-begotten before all creatures,' or 'the firstborn of every creation.' The thought is in perfect harmony with other expressions in scripture, e.g. (a) Rom. 8 [19ff]. Here all creation from the lowest to the highest is described as lifting up its head in hope from the groanings which are themselves the prophecies of a completeness to come. It is to Christ all things look for the revelation of the meaning which is bound up in the age-long struggle, and for the glory which is life's true goal. (b) Rev. 4 [66] gives us that remarkable picture, reflected in Jan Van Eych's famous Altar piece of Ghent, where all circles of created things bow in adoration around the 'Lamb, slain from the foundation of the world.' Here the Four Living Ones proclaim the confidence of universal Nature that the Love of God, displayed in the sacrifice of Christ, offers adequate explanation of the purpose and end of created life. Putting together such passages as these, passages which lay the foundation for the only reverent and comprehensive conception of Natural Science, we are able in the following verses to summarize what Paul would here emphasize for the Colossian Christians, as for all men of all ages.

(viii) Some of the early opponents of Arius gave to πρωτότοκος, against all known usage, an active sense: 'First-*begetter* of all creation.' Athanasius and other Greek Fathers of the fourth century, in the stress of the same controversy, were led to propound what subsequently became the standard Socinian interpretation, understanding 'creation' to mean 'the new (moral) creation.' This is against the whole scope of the context, and cuts the nerve of Paul's argument. The current Jewish theosophy distributed the offices of representing God, and of mediating between Him and the creatures, amongst a variable and wholly nebulous crowd of agencies: Angels, Words, Powers, neither human nor strictly divine. Paul gathers all these mediatorial and administrative functions into one, and places them firmly in the hands of 'the Son of His love.' Looking up to God, Christ is the Image. Looking down on creation, Christ is its primal Head and Lord. 'Creation,' standing collectively without the article in antithesis to 'Firstborn,' is used qualitatively (cf. verse 23 and *Eph.* 2 [21]). This is more satisfactory than making κτίσις a quasi-proper noun, or rendering distributively 'every creature'. Paul's reasoning is perfectly just, for the *creation* of all things (*Col.* 1 [16]) and *the making* of the world (*Heb.* 1 [3]) *through the Son*, is a direct proof that He is the firstborn, heir, and Lord of the whole. For the same reason, in verse 18 πρωτότοκος 'firstborn' may signify Lord or Ruler; especially if the verse is translated 'He is the beginning, the firstborn of the dead.'

To return to the main theme. Whilst, on the one hand, we may regard this cosmic range as the sublimest aspect of Christ's work, we must not fall into the temptation so rife to-day of denigrating man as a 'sick fly,' a 'bit of cosmic mud,' and so on. It is becoming increasingly common amongst our writers to-day to emphasize the insignificance of man as an infinitesimal fragment of the universe, and that therefore it is absurd to attribute to him the importance which the Christian religion attaches to him. But the saving work of Christ is not simply an adjunct of a larger world-embracing function which Christ had to fulfil. Paul certainly regarded Christ as the active agent of the Godhead concerning the whole Creation (as also did St. John), but he also kept things in their true relation, for his system of the universe is neither geo-centric nor helio-centric but Christo-centric, not merely material but essentially spiritual. If, therefore, the whole Creation benefits by the work of Christ, as indeed it does, it is still only as a sequel and corollary to the benefit obtained by mankind. It is all for a redeemed humanity.

(b) CHRIST'S RELATION TO THE UNIVERSE. I 16-17

Exposition

This brings us to Paul's summary. First, Christ establishes the *Unity of Creation*. Thus there can be no such thing in the Cosmos as anarchy. All realms of Nature are held together by the Divine Presence. The true genealogy of Christ reaches back not merely to the Jew, but, as even the Jewish Gospel of St. Matthew reminds us, through the Jew to foreigners like Rahab and Ruth and Bathsheba; back indeed to primitive man, to the anthropoid ape, to the proto-plasm which first stirred with life from God. Caliban, as well as David, is the ancestor of Jesus, the Piltdown Man as well as Plato, the 'Voice that breathed o'er Eden' as well as the Voice of Him who 'spake as never man spake.' Expel, if you will, the Divine intervention in the story of the Annunciation of the Blessed Virgin Mary; but you are obliged to admit it at the starting of the line. Whatever gaps may lie between, the words 'which was the son of Adam' necessitate at last the final link 'which was the Son of God.' Secondly, Christ interprets for us the *Universal Experience of Nature*. He enables us to understand not only the sufferings of Hiroshima and Nagasaki, and the horrors of German concentration camps, and the shatterings of Warsaw, and the shudderings of Hungary, and the oppressions of Tibet, but also the sufferings of the brute creation all the way from the modern slaughterhouses to the time when the dragons dismembered each other in the primeval slime. The claim of Amid: 'Where the gnat cries, there am I,' is much more essentially Christian than it is Buddhist. St. Francis was not going beyond the scope of his evangel in preaching to the birds and fishes and in his extraordinary pacification of the wolf of Gubbio. It was not weak sentiment that moved Ralph Hodgson to write:

'Twould ring the bells of Heaven,
The wildest peal for years,
If parson lost his senses
And people came to theirs;
And he and they together
Knelt down with angry prayers
For tamed and shabby tigers,
And dancing dogs and bears,
And wretched blind pit-ponies,
And little hunted hares.

Thirdly, Christ establishes the *Essential Goodness of the Universe*, considered not in its present stage of imperfection or incompleteness, but in the light of that glory which is to be revealed. In other words, as we are expected to see men *non quales sumus, sed quales futuri sumus*, so we are to judge even this present 'naughty world' in the light of the completed redemption yet to be. Very much of the present-day cynical and often hypocritical depreciation of this world would be corrected, and become impossible, if only we were continuously expectant through Christ of that great Climax of evolution which is to justify the existence of things material as well as of 'things to come.' Whether we accept the evolutionary theory of cosmology or that of continuous creation, the whole mysterious order (which looks more like a multiverse, with its myriads of galaxies) becomes a real universe by becoming Christo-centric. It is revealed as being 'in Him' because He is its creative centre. It is also 'through Him' that it is carried onward to its goal by 'the Love that moves the sun and th'other stars.' It is 'unto Him' as perceiving in Him its ultimate goal. Seen thus, all things cohere in Him who holds up with His pierced hands the whole Creation. And it is all created things which the *Benedicite* in the Book of Common Prayer exhorts to praise the Author of their being, their Divine Source and Ground and Inner Purpose.

Although Paul is said to have taken over the apocalyptic view of the world from the primitive Gospel, and shares with Jesus the current belief in angels, satan, and the demons and their sway over the world and man, and creation's 'bondage to corruption' (*Rom.* 8 [20ff]), from which both nature and humanity are impotent to free themselves, evil is not omnipotent or independent of God: 'the earth is the Lord's and all the fullness thereof' (1 *Cor.* 10 [26]); therefore Christ's *cosmic function* is concerned with the ultimate realization of the Divine Rule. Redemption and Reconciliation include all things in heaven and earth.

The special feature here is that Christ is represented as the Ideal and Goal of the Creation. Not only does Redemption centre in Him, but also the World, the Universe, the whole Cosmos. He is not only 'the Head of the Church' (which the Church of to-day continually emphasizes) but of Humanity, of all Creation (which is a fact much neglected). Redemption through Christ is not an after-thought of God, but the outcome of an 'eternal Purpose' in which the universe itself was founded. There is not only a Divine purpose *in* the Creation, but also *for* it. That Ideal was the Christ '*in* whom all things were created,' and it is as the realization of that Ideal that Christ appears. There are not two separate Divine movements, one represented by Creation and the other by Redemption; there is but *one* movement, natural and spiritual, issuing in both. The Christ who appears as Redeemer existed eternally in the thought and purpose of God. He does not enter the world for the first time in what is called the Incarnation; His appearance is the outcome of a Divine creative process in its fullness, not to be separated from it; the Incarnation is the fullness in manifestation of the Divine creative act, and at the same time of the Creator. The personal life of Christ was the expression in time of that which is eternal in God. This conception of Christ's Person alone satisfies reason as well as faith and makes our theology at one with science. Science sees the Universe as a mighty *organism*, evolving, developing—but to what end? Surely as the expression of *Perfect Love*; as the fulfilment of the Divine Intention for Humanity which is still striving towards God's ideal of universal and perfected benevolence. Christianity has been the first to recognize the spiritual as well as the rational ground of the Universe. Accordingly, the Divine *Logos*, by which is meant the Eternal Reason, Meaning, and ground of all Creation, is one. Thus, if Jesus Christ is the Logos of man, then He is the Logos of all creation (of what we now call Evolution) of which man is the final cause and crown. If, therefore, He is the Logos of these, He is also the Logos of God Himself. That is to say, the full account of Man is the account of the Universe, so far as it has significance for us, and the truth of the Universe and of Man as its end and crown expresses all the account God can give us of Himself. And He has perfectly expressed it in the Person of Christ Jesus as the Ideal of Creation itself. In Him alone can we be perfected.

Paul thus interprets Christ in terms of the *anima mundi*. Without Him nothing could exist. He is the Principle in which all created things find their unity and meaning. He is the Source of the world's life, the Centre of all its development, the Mainspring of all its motions. Thus the created world derives its being and existence through that mighty act of God's love which we call the Creation. In Christ that initial creative act, impaired by the emergence of man's wilful refusal to obey the Divine Purpose for his life, is both rectified and completed. Creation is *spiritualized*, and man's life is set in the spaciousness of the supernatural. Man's life is no longer enslaved by 'cosmic powers.' All things owe allegiance to Him. Observe Paul's mounting thought in verse 16—*In Him* carries us back to the beginning of creation: *through Him* leads us along its process: *unto Him* points us to the end and the abiding result.

Although Paul is deeply concerned about the mythological and theosophical interpretations of the cosmological ideas current in his day, together with the deifications of the principles of law and order as perceived in the forces of nature, he perceives an infinitely larger Mystery. He realizes that the Christian faith is concerned with more than man's redemption; indeed that must be co-ordinated with the highest possible conceptions of the Universe, and that in Christ we must seek for its ultimate meaning. Thus Christ is more than the agent of man's redemption; He is the agent of Creation itself and the Sustainer of the World. Without Him the Universe, like Man himself, is bereft of Purpose, Meaning, Divine Intention.

(c) CHRIST'S RELATION TO THE CHURCH. I [18]

He is the Head of the Body, the Church. Paul now proceeds to the consideration of Christ as the Head of the Church, which is called 'the Body of Christ,' because all the regenerated are united to Him and to each other by His Incarnation, His sacrificial death, and His wondrous Resurrection 'for us men and for our salvation, and for our justification.' The Church is not *a* body of Christians, it is *the* Body of Christ. We are on extremely important ground here, the more so at a time when the doctrine of The Church has become one of the most important of all theological issues. So important indeed, that it has been called 'the great vacuum in Christian theology.'

The first thing to remember, in dealing with the Pauline conception of the Church, is that Paul's language is by no means uniform, since he describes the Church under many metaphors: the Bride of the Lamb, the Temple of the Spirit, the Household of God, God's husbandry, and the Body of Christ. Paul apparently considers all these terms as necessary to his purpose, each incomplete in itself, but each indicating a distinct reality, definite and particular. In fact the Pauline doctrine of the Church presents a kind of double thesis in some respects self-contradictory, not because Paul intended to convey two different sets of truths but because he wanted to apply the same truth in two different ways. And this is seen quite clearly in the Body-metaphor as used in the Romans-1 Corinthians thesis, and in the Ephesians-Colossians thesis. The idea of the Church as the Body of Christ is developed more specifically in Ephesians[1] where it receives its fruitful application. In Colossians the doctrine of the Person of Christ and the doctrine of the Church find their meeting-point as mutually implying each other, and together opposed to the double effect of early Gnosticism which tended first to lower the dignity of Christ, and then to impair the unity of His Church (cf. 2 [19]). In I Cor. 12 [12-27] and Rom. 12 [4-5] the figure of 'the Body and members' is merely a passing illustration of the mutual relation of believers in the Church; now 'the Body of Christ' becomes the formal title of the Church, expressing the fundamental conception of its nature as related to Him who is the Centre of its unity, the Nucleus and Source of all its life and energy, and directing

---

[1] See *Studies in Ephesians*, ch. 5, by S. F. B. Bedale (Mowbray, 1956).

control within it (cf. the Vine and the branches, *John* 15). Thus the expression of the life of Christ through His Body is teleological, and its *telos* is that the whole Body should grow up into the 'fullness' of Christ. That is the teaching of Ephesians-Colossians, while that of Romans-1 Corinthians is that the complete life of Christ is expressed by being articulated in a distinct manner through each member for the benefit of the whole. In Romans-1 Corinthians the process is extensive; in Ephesians-Colossians it is intensive. But it is all one and the same process of growth. In simple words, what Paul is trying to teach is that the Fullness of Christ is diversified through the members of the body so that the whole body should grow up into that Fullness.

This requires further consideration: If Christ, as the revelation of God, draws all things downward from the Pleroma to Himself, and if, as the revelation of Nature, He draws all things upward, even from the Abyss, to Him, the circle described from such a Centre, with so remarkable a radius above and below, must mark for us the completeness of that Body in which Christ is All in all. Christ is the *Head* of that Body, not merely as the source of all authority, but also as the source of all life. Consequently, the Christian may not properly regard Christ primarily as the Teacher even though He be 'a teacher come from God,' for then must the Christian be mainly occupied with learning what Christ taught rather than what He is. Nor is he to think of Christ primarily as the Example, since in this case Religion would be for the most part an imitation of what Christ did. But Christianity is primarily Life. He is the Head of the Body, not in the sense of being first in a series, as was Muhammad in relation to the Kalifs, but as being the First Principle. He is *Principium principians*, not *principium principiatum*. His life is the pledge of ours. The Body, with all its members, is infused with the immortality of the Head.

There are three movements summarized by Paul: (1) We have the revelation of the Father in the Son which, starting from the fact of God's transcendence, expresses all history in terms of the Devolution or Condescension of God. The climax to this process is the Christ, the *Son of God*. (2) The ascent of Creation which, starting from the fact of God's immanence, expresses the selfsame history in terms of the Evolution of Nature. To this process the climax is the Christ, the *Son of Man*. (3) No longer must the Universe

be conceived as an Eternal Dualism wherein so-called Matter forever remains subject to the realm of Darkness, and God is thus
excluded from one half of the whole, but as one Infinite Realm,
the Ideal Church, in which the power of the Cross extends 'higher
than the highest heaven, deeper than the deepest hell,' and represents
the victory of the height and depth and breadth of the Almighty
and Eternal Love.

Thus Christ is the *fons et origo* of the Church, as of all else. The
Church is integral to the *Pleroma*, and in Him it finds its completion.
He is not only the central principle of the Universe; He is also the
Head of the Church from which the Church draws its life which
animates the organic whole. That is precisely what the Ideal
Church is intended to be. But is it so? Is it so to-day? Is it a Body
in which there are no divisions? There is nothing in scripture which
contemplates as legitimate or necessary a divided state of the Church,
such as we are familiar with to-day. Everywhere in the Word of
God the Church is 'one body,' one in spirit and one in fellowship.
All believers are fully enfranchized in this one body. And if indeed
the Church is truly the Body of Christ, how could it be otherwise?
'There is one Body and one Spirit, even as ye are called in one hope
of your calling: one Lord, one Faith, one Baptism, one God and
Father of all. . . . It thus becomes foolish and sinful to say, "I am of
Paul, and I of Apollos, and I of Cephas, and I of Christ." ' Even if a
spiritual unity existed among all Christians, there could be no valid
reason why division in the visible Church should be regarded, as
it is by so many, as a matter of little moment. Spiritual unity should
represent and complete itself in visible form, and were it perfect it
would undoubtedly do so. The present variety of Churches finds
its analogue, it is said, in the variety of members in the human body,
or in the different regiments in an army. If this and similar views are
correct, it is singular that the New Testament does not recognize
it in any place. There is not a single hint as to forming distinct
communions to accommodate diversities in doctrine, temperament,
or rank in society. The idea of 'hiving' persons in separate communions according to such diversities finds no support in the New
Testament, and is alien to the genius of Christianity. It cannot be
that the Church's Head assigns to one 'denomination' of His
followers the duty of emphasizing the Sovereignty of God, to
another the duty of proclaiming the freedom of man and the

principles of Human Rights; appoints one communion to minister to the intellect in the clear apprehension of doctrinal truths, another to adapt its services to the fluctuating demands of the passing hour; one to enforce the message of salvation by grace, another to declare the necessity of good works, and yet another to insist upon sacramental confession before being permitted to 'draw near with faith and take this holy Sacrament to your comfort.' It is the duty of the Church to set forth 'the whole counsel of God,' all the elements of divine truth, to every person. For any denomination to claim, or deliberately to say, that it proposes to attend to certain aspects of the work which Christ the Head entrusted to His members is exceedingly like proclaiming itself to be something much less than the Church of Christ. Any Church that is organized under any narrower view than the faithful discharge of the whole work committed to the Christian Church as the Body of Christ is setting before itself an aim that must necessarily be declared essentially defective. Allowing for all the inevitable differences in human beings, it ought to be possible to achieve the real Unity of the Church. If indeed the Church is to be effective in our modern world, it must strive unceasingly to become *one*, remembering that 'unto each one of us was given grace'—the personal, individual, gift that constitutes specific capacity for effective membership in the one Body— according to the measure of the gift of Christ.' The unity is not one of a humanly created organization and authority. It is rather the internal unity of the Spirit. No humanly organized church, nor any number of such churches, can form the complete Body of Christ, which in its very nature must embrace all who are vitally united to Christ. Ideally, the Church embraces humanity. Therefore, no humanly organized body can ever be commensurate with it. But the unity is not an ideal only, but is meant to be absolute in reality and influence. A divided body is an imperfect conception. The essential bond of union is a spiritual union; it consists not in any one organization, but in a common principle of life. The Church is not an organization at all; it is an organism. The unity of the Spirit means, therefore, much more than a union of churches, or even a formal union of all Christians. Indeed a union of churches might be no more effective than a union of churchyards. Living, active love is the hallmark of the true Christian; and where this is wanting the churches are as cold as the grave. 'By this shall all men

know that ye are My disciples, if ye have love one to another.'
was through the manifestation of Christian unity in this love tha
the world was to believe. And it was this that so deeply impresse
the pagan world. The love that was expressed was seen to b
the Love that God is. But we know how soon the spiritual concep
tion of the Church was lost, and how an outward uniformity unde
humanly constituted authority became substituted for the Churc
of the Spirit. Even now, despite all ecumenical endeavours, thi
high conception of the Church is too feebly embraced by man
Churches and Christians. Churches too frequently appear to b
'institutions' with interests of their own to advance and private end
to pursue, while the great end for which the Church was called int
being is comparatively little heeded. So the masses are visibl
drifting away from all religion, because Christianity has come to b
regarded as a particular thing belonging to some particular churcl
instead of a universal Spirit of Love which influences and embrace
all human life in all its aspects and activities, the expression of th
Greatest Thing in the World—*that* by which the world should b
redeemed, uplifted, sanctified, perfected, and blessed in all its rela
tionships, as God seeks to bless it as men are united in the one tru
life as a real family of God.

It is this view of the Church that needs to be restored to th
people of our time. The Christ-life which should fill the Churcl
and permeate the world is not a life in separation from the ordinar
life of men and women living in this present world. It is that sam
life under its highest inspiration, in its truest form, directed to it
supremest end—a *higher* life than that which normally animates ou
humanity, but not a *different* life. It is human life lifted to its highes
term, with all that is unworthy of Christ forever left behind. I
other words it is the life of the Living Christ Himself diffusing itsel
in the world according to the Eternal Purpose and Divine Ideal o
God in Creation.

But the Church has come to be regarded as a *separate* thing that i
aloof from the world, while others are doing the work the Churcl
is supposed to do. The religion that the instincts of men are callin
for to-day is an all-embracing one: Divine indeed it must be, abov
the level of the worldly-world, yet genuinely human in the highe
sense, looking to the temporal interests of men as God's children
and covering the whole range of human life. In short, what mer

nd women most earnestly seek to-day in relation to the Church is
. full manifestation of an effective practice of the Christian life—
nd Christians as the salt of the earth, the light of the world, the
amp that is placed on the lampstand to give light to all around,
;lorifying God through good deeds. True doctrine, faithful exposi-
ion, church organizations, societies, sodalities, brotherhoods, unions,
neticulous performance of ritualistic niceties—all these may be very
;ood in themselves, but these alone will never move the world for
Christ. They may satisfy those within, but they will not have any
nfluence upon those that are without. It is the good life and the
;ood deeds that will the more certainly impress and gain them for
God and His Christ. Jesus does not spare His members the experience
of heroic and sacrificial living. To be a Christian means above all
lse to be like Christ. That involves a Cross. Redemptive love for
Christ's sake may not feed the fires of our modern statistical mania;
ts gains are not likely to be spectacular; but its power would reach
eyond all human calculation; it would rescue religion from the
eeble hands of institutions that are either moribund with too much
:omplacency, or cursed with too much academic irrelevance.
We shall not 'build Jerusalem in England's green and pleasant
and' by merely repairing our church fabric, necessary as that may
e: our first need is to make all Churches more Christian, more
Holy, more truly Catholic as a *given* unity, as the Body of Christ
ver meeting the costliest demands of redeeming love on the
iniversal scale. But all this calls for immense sacrifice, and the
juestion at once arises: have we lost the capacity for sacrifice?
Do we lack the moral discrimination and the spiritual discernment
hat reveals the things most worthy of sacrifice? It may well be
hat our modern Calvaries are less redemptive than they might be,
ecause they are less sacrificial than they should be. We have
villingly sacrificed millions of lives for war, but we are nervously
eluctant about sacrificing nuclear tests for the sake of peace. The
esult is that our Calvaries enfold us in still deeper darkness. The
Church will become more Christian, more Holy, and more
Catholic when we determine at all cost to live for the things and
ralues for which Jesus died, and die for everything He lived for.
he Church will then be Christ's effective instrument for the salva-
ion of the world, and man will be transformed into the likeness of

that Divine image which is set before us in Him. Meantime th
increase of the Body must be the building up of itself in love.

(d) THE FULLNESS OF CHRIST'S GODHEAD. *Paul's doctrine of th '*Pleroma.' I [19]

For it pleased the Father that in Christ all the plenitude of Deity shoul make its dwelling, without limit.

The point which Paul is making here is that in Christ dwel
all the forces and laws of the *first* creation, and that also in Hin
dwells 'all the Fullness' engaged in the *new* creation. We are, how
ever, faced with a difficult problem of interpretation. *Pleroma* is
word so varied and elastic in Paul's usage that it can scarcely hav
hardened into what Lightfoot called 'a recognized term in theology
denoting the totality of the Divine Person and attributes.' No earlie
example of such a usage is furnished, and to import it here is to mak
the Epistle speak the language of the second century.

'All the fullness' ascribed to 'the Son of God's love' as 'Head ove
all things to the Church,' alike 'Beginning of God's creation' and
'Firstborn out of the dead,' embraces that entire plenitude of natur
and the power residing in Him since His ascension to the right hand
of power, in virtue of which He becomes 'in all things pre-eminent.
From henceforth Christ is a *complete* Christ, and we are 'made
complete in Him' (2 [9-10]). This plenitude qualifies Him as pleni
potentiary in His work of reconciliation.

This is perhaps the simplest paraphrase possible of Paul's tremen
dous but triumphant assertion of the presence of the *Pleroma* here
and now in Christ through whom God has drawn near to man
'All the Fullness,' the perfect totality of the Godhead, the plenitude
of Deity, dwells permanently and perfectly (such is the force of the
word *katoikei*) in Him, in His own Person. There is no need for the
would-be saint to climb up into heaven in order to lie prostrate
before God's Throne and gaze upon the glory of the Beatific
Vision. The heaven in which God dwells lies all around 'the sons of
God,' closer than breathing, nearer than hands and feet.

Christian faith cannot rest content with a merely historically-
manifested Christ, a brilliant Light that shone for a few brief years
but finally quenched, a Personality in whom God was clearly seen
while it lasted but which has now passed forever beyond our reach.

Christian faith holds a present relation to Christ as the living Lord and Saviour, Christ is still God-with-us. Christ is not only 'He in whom all things were created' and all things also brought back to God; but as representing man in his truth at-one-with God, He becomes a new Divine-human Head to the whole race in receiving whom as such alone can it find its full true life or become a divinely-ordered Body. *Completeness* is the outstanding fact of the essential nature of God in Christ, not merely temporarily dwelling in Christ, but absolutely and permanently, substantially and personally in Himself, and in His Body the Church. The whole fullness of the Godhead has become concentrated in Him in that form in which the Divine Life seeks to live in and fill us and make us eternally His very own. It is in Him that the Divine Purpose for Humanity has realized itself as in a representative man who becomes the new Divine-human Head of the race, the source of the fullness of the higher eternal life of sonship. 'In Him ye are made full.' This is likewise true of the Church.

This carries us back to the thought of the Eternal Sonship in God as being that in which the Creation was conceived, now fully realized in Christ, and opens out before us the highest conceivable prospect for man. If God was so incarnated in Christ as to form one undivided Personality, human and Divine, the laying aside of the physical body freed that Personality from all corporeal limitations, so that He could be with His Church (His avowed and dedicated Christians) in a more intimate and abiding manner. He is now not only 'all' but also '*in* all', as the Life Eternal.

Not only is there no limit to His Spiritual Presence, but He has realized in Himself all that belongs to man's spiritual and eternal life. The whole Divine Fullness dwells in Him, and He is able out of it to impart to every man that which he needs in his desire for the achievement of that Ideal of which, and for which, he was created. But only by faith in Him do we stand in the Christian succession. Until His *pleroma* is found in the Church, His presence and work in the world are incomplete.

(e) RECONCILIATION IN CHRIST. I [20-23]

The theology of Paul is concerned largely with Salvation, the salvation of man and the universe, as a universal salvation. In the background of his system of salvation are the concepts of sin, law, and judgement. There is the broad fact of the universality of sin as a thing that *reigns*, disrupting the whole world and bringing the soul of every man into servitude, culminating in death. There is no human way of escape from sin. Man is caught in the toils of his iniquity and can find no remedy. All he can do is to cry out in the anguish of his despair, 'O wretched man that I am! Who shall deliver me from the body of this death?' Paul's view of human impotence belongs to the region of fact rather than of dogma. When Aristotle, at the commencement of his Ethics, said that 'a man who was still the slave of passion would listen to his arguments in vain and derive no profit from them,' he was stating in other language the doctrine of St. Paul. Aristotle is quite as emphatic as Paul in saying that he knows no means of making the bad man good. The impotence of man in the presence of evil is a fact universally recognized by honest interpreters of human nature.

But sin is something more with Paul than a question of impotence. Nor is sin something that destroys character and makes moral wrecks. It is a far worse evil than that. Sin stands as an impassable barrier between man and God. It breaks the true relationship, and puts man 'under wrath.' It means the loss of everything for him in this world and beyond. The real problem for Paul is 'How can a man be just before God?' Our modern world is much too ready to accept the boastful utterance of a French philosopher, 'I have abolished sin'; but the greatest minds of all ages have been far more in sympathy with the Pauline position than with the shallow attitude of some present-day thinkers. Paul's anguish of heart finds its counterpart in the religious development of an Augustine, a Luther, a Wesley, a Whitfield, and a Bunyan, to mention but a few.

God's law, having been broken, judgement ensues. Hence the emergence of Paul's antithesis of sin and righteousness, of law and grace, of wrath and salvation, of condemnation and justification, of sin and sanctification, of judgement and redemption, of terror and peace. Instead of fear is gladness, for all antinomies are solved, and all bliss is secured in the Gospel of Christ. The answer to Paul's problem was found in the grace of God in Jesus Christ. Christ was not only 'the power of God unto salvation,' the power which transformed human impotence into moral strength, the power which gave man the victory over sin, but He also completely broke down the barrier which sin had created between man and God, restored the relationship which it had destroyed, and brought pardon and peace to the stricken soul. Christ sets men right with God, and provides for the progressive development of the soul in righteousness. Christ is the Reconciler, and the term Reconciliation is in itself a most comprehensive doctrinal conception. It assumes the existence of a state of enmity between man and God, the result of persistent disobedience and the universality of sin. But it also implies the removal of that enmity, and the establishment of peace with God. Further, it contains the promise and potency of a 'new life,' a life of unblemished holiness and unmarred happiness. In brief, the whole Christian revelation is in 'the reconciliation,' and the work of Christ is exhaustively described in the words, 'God was in Christ, reconciling the world unto Himself, not imputing unto them their trespasses.' The apostolic message to man and the world alike is 'the word of reconciliation.' The Greek word used by Paul means 'to harmonize that which is discordant: to take back into favour: to unite.' For Paul, the Gospel is 'the mystery of Christ which has been hidden from all the ages and is now revealed.' Christ has accomplished God's determinate will to comprise or sum up all things in heaven and earth in Him as their Head, in the fullness of the times. This is the Divine dispensation of things, which is Paul's way of expressing the 'reconciliation of all things.' This reconciliation to Christ-the-King also concerns the 'all things' of verse 16, restoring in Himself the broken unity of Creation, broken by sin. This the Father has done by 'making peace' between Himself and sinful men, and sinful men to one another, through the blood of His Son's cross. In other words, the whole disrupted Creation both material and spiritual, and the whole disunited human race of every nation and tongue, are to be united to Him and one another by the all-sufficing mediation of Christ which alone creates that condition of peace in which all enmity is abolished and harmony restored. The initiative is God's, by whom the basis of redemption is provided, and from whom the call goes forth as a message of love, calling on man to yield. Man's former self-chosen alienation had shown itself in both mental and moral evil. But with Paul, alienation is not and cannot be one-sided: there is another alienation which denotes not a subjective feeling on the part of the sinner but an objective determination on the part of God, an exclusion from

F

Divine favour, from the Kingdom of the Son, from the lot of the
saints. But Christ has effected a complete salvation which none but
He could do, namely, 'by the blood of His cross.'

Reconciliation rests on expiation. The Pauline terms—sin, law
guilt, judgement, death—are not rhetorical. The law pertains to a
holy and righteous God, and there is inherent within it a judgement-
principle, a 'curse.' The idea of Omar Khayyam, 'Pish! he's a good
fellow, and 'twill all be well,' finds no part in the thought of Paul.
To him, as to his race, sin is a terrible thing that must be atoned for,
and man escapes the terrible consequences only because Christ bore
the curse of the law (*Gal.* 3 [13]). Thus an atoning death is implicit,
and only the sufferings of a Divine Person could be sufficiently
precious to be efficacious for a world steeped in sin. It was Paul's
intense consciousness of sin and guilt which issued in his profound
doctrine of deliverance from sin as from all conditions of mortality.
Christ's transcendant act in the restoration of humanity to its birthright in God was the sacrifice upon the cross and His resurrecton
from the dead. In Paulinism the two are inseparable. 'In the body of
His flesh through death' emphasizes the fact that the material body
of Jesus is made the instrument of reconciliation in the carrying out
of which 'His whole Fullness' is engaged. Here was a corrective
of the Alexandrian-Jewish philosophy with its contempt for matter
and physical life generally, which was just beginning to leaven the
Church. Paul's argument is that it was for the redemption of the
body-of-sin that Christ assumed a sinless body-of-flesh in His
incarnation.

Much trouble has arisen from the confusion of *sarx* with *soma*.
Sarx, though liable to entertain sin, was not from the first inherently
evil: it was the Hellenistic view which taught that *sarx* was 'wholly
evil.' Thus the doctrine of 'the Word made flesh' was indeed a
stumbling-block to those who could not conceive of the Deity
taking sinful flesh. Paul, however, accepted the Incarnation without
qualification. Christ indeed had *sarx*, a body of flesh, but not of sin-
yielding flesh. In Christ the life of the flesh achieved its highest
possibility in absolute freedom from sin. That sinless body was
crucified on Calvary by sin for sin's redemption, and only a perfect
offering was in itself sufficient from that holy purpose. And it was
the sinless body which Christ took again at the Resurrection and
which in His Ascension He gave back to God from whom it took its

origin, for man's 'justification.' This is the faith, claims Paul, which alone can withstand every shock, every onslaught, that would carry men away from, or shatter their faith in, 'the hope of the Gospel.'

The revelation of the *Fullness* is also the *Reconciliation*, since henceforth and for ever is abolished the long frontier between the Material and the Spiritual. Christ is the Eternal Word, Centre of a new universe in which 'all things' find place in one redeeming plan. That is Paul's word to the Colossians, and it is not less the Word of God to ourselves to-day. Now as then it is a great emancipating thought which would, if we gave full heed to it, carry us victoriously through all the doubts and disasters of this mid-twentieth century, even as St. Patrick's *Breastplate* carried that glorious saint through all the moors and fogs and forests of pagan Erin—

> Christ be with me, Christ within me,
> Christ behind me, Christ before me,
> Christ beside me, Christ to win me,
> Christ to comfort and restore me,
> Christ beneath me, Christ above me,
> Christ in quiet, Christ in danger,
> Christ in hearts of all that love me,
> Christ in mouth of friend and stranger.
>
> I bind unto myself the Name,
> The strong Name of the Trinity;
> By invocation of the same,
> The three in one, and one in three.
> Of whom all nature hath Creation;
> Eternal Father, Spirit, Word:
> Praise to the Lord of my salvation,
> Salvation is of Christ the Lord.

SECTION 3. A PARENTHESIS BY WAY OF PERSONAL EXPLANATION CONCERNING PAUL HIMSELF AND HIS MISSION

Authorized Version   *Translation*

THE REVELATION OF THE MYSTERY.   I 24-29

24 Who now rejoice in my sufferings for you, and fill up that which is behind of the afflictions of Christ in my flesh for his body's sake, which is the church:

24 Now I rejoice in my sufferings for your sakes, and in my turn fill up the full sum of all the afflictions which Christ must suffer in my body for the sake of His Body, which is the Church,—

25 Whereof I am made a minister, according to the dispensation of God which is given to me for you, to fulfil the word of God;

26 *Even* the mystery which hath been hid from ages and from generations, but now is made manifest to his saints:

27 To whom God would make known what *is* the riches of the glory of this mystery among the Gentiles; which is Christ in you, the hope of glory:

28 Whom we preach, warning every man, and teaching every man in all wisdom; that we may present every man perfect in Christ Jesus:

29 Whereunto I also labour, striving according to his working, which worketh in me mightily.

25 whereof I am made a minister according to the dispensation of God, which was given to me on your account, fully to preach the word of God—

26 namely, of that Mystery which was concealed from past ages and generations, but is now disclosed to His saints—

27 to whom God willed to make known what is the riches of the glory of this Mystery, which is Christ in you, the Hope of Glory:

28 the Christ whom we preach; admonishing every man, and teaching every man with all wisdom, that we may present every man perfect in Christ Jesus:

29 For which end I labour, combating vigorously according to the effectual working of Him who works effectually in me with dynamic energy.

Exposition

The great mystery of human life itself is now revealed, and Paul is in prison for having preached it, namely Salvation for the Gentiles equally with the Jews through the sacrificial death of Christ on Calvary's Cross. Lest the fact of imprisonment might lead the Colossians to suspect the truth of his doctrine and of himself as a fraud, Paul assures them that he rejoices in the afflictions he is enduring for their sakes in maintaining their title to salvation, and that these afflictions are expressly appointed to him by the Living Christ for the purpose of building up the Church. Paul's body, naturally afflicted, is now further afflicted for the sake of Christ's Body (verse 24), of which Body, namely the Church, he tells them a second time that he was made a minister to build it up by publishing God's determination to save the believing Gentiles (verse 25). He then proceeds to inform them that this plan or purpose is indeed a Mystery, a secret, which, during the Mosaic dispensation was kept hidden from Jew and Gentile alike, but is now disclosed to such of the Jews as God thinks fit to employ in proclaiming it to all the world (verse 26) through Paul and his fellow-preachers. God is pleased to reveal to all men the amazing splendour of that Mystery, namely that to the Gentiles also the Lord Christ is the author of a glorious resurrection to eternal life, as well as to the Jews (verse 27). Christ is the Saviour of the world. Paul exhorts every man to receive Him as a personal redeemer. With God-given wisdom Paul would teach every man the true doctrines of this revealed Religion, so that at the last 'every man may be presented perfect in Christ Jesus' (verse 26). In order to accomplish that great purpose, Paul himself labours with unabated endeavour in preaching Christ as 'the Hope of Glory' to all the believers of all the nations, and in defending that doctrine with success proportionate to the super-natural gifts bestowed upon him in his Apostleship (verse 29).

Christ the Head has borne His part, once offered upon Calvary's Cross, once and once for all. Now Paul in his turn fills up his part in the total sum of suffering to be undergone on behalf of Christ's Body, the Church. Paul does not mean that Christ's sufferings are inadequate and incomplete, needing to be supplemented by addi-tional sufferings in order to render them effectual. The phrase 'afflictions of Christ', being the genitive of the agent, signifies not the afflictions which Christ Himself suffered, but those which He appointed Paul to suffer in building up the Church. 'I will show him what things he must suffer for My Name's sake.' Therefore Paul must, at all cost to mind, body, and spirit, make his own full contribution to the total suffering which Christ's Body must undergo in its earthly warfare against the powers of evil. And warfare means wounds. Does not every truly dedicated minister of Christ, from the youngest deacon newly ordained to the oldest missionary in the field, share this dominating desire 'to suffer and to die' for Christ and His Church? But this must never be interpreted as meaning or even remotely suggesting that the sufferings of the saints are so meritorious as to procure easy pardons for others. The sacrifice of Christ is the sole meritorious ground of salvation. But the Christian is called upon to take up *his* Cross, not as something thrust upon him, but humbly and thankfully for voluntary suffering 'for Christ's sake and the Gospel's.'

It is important to observe that Paul never uses the words 'suffer,' 'suffering,' 'affliction,' in connection with the atoning sacrifice; but rather dwells on the objective fact itself, namely 'the death,' 'the cross,' 'the blood.' Paul makes it clear that he rejoices in the purpose for which he suffers for the Church, not for the sake of procuring pardon for the Church but as an unchallengeable proof of his sincerity in teaching the salvation of the Gentiles through faith, whereby the faith of believers in every age is strengthened and perfected.

Thus Paul can claim that he has preached the full Gospel of Christ. He has proclaimed the Gospel message in all its fullness, namely that one mighty truth which is the very heart of it—the revelation of that Mystery which was concealed from former generations but is now disclosed openly to all believers, a Mystery which concerns the whole human race freed from all racial exclusiveness in whatever form. No revelation, no discovery, can be more welcome. It emphasizes the unique relation in which Christ stands to the human race. This is truly the world's 'Hope of Glory.' Christ is the manifestation of man in his true life. Every man of every race and clime and colour is to become like Him. He is the living embodiment of an ideal humanity, destined to influence all times by lifting every man coming into the world to the measure of His stature. His is the life towards which all men are to be moved even in the course of natural Evolution, the life in which alone all men can be brothers, and humanity can become that united family which is God's determinate purpose. The destiny of the human race is revealed in Christ alone. *Apartheid* anywhere is a terrible wrong, a satanic challenge to the Divine purpose. It is integrated with the dark Mystery of evil itself.

But there is a greater Mystery—that man's divinely intended destiny is summed up in one word, *Glory*; that all men were created for Sonship to Almighty God and for an inheritance in His Eternal and perfected Kingdom. Man was not made for merely earthly joy or sorrow, nor to be the sport of circumstance, nor to be crushed at length under the unbending necessities of the laws of matter, nor for death and nothingness. He was made for Glory, for the glorious wealth which this Mystery holds. God's love in Christ is itself the profoundest of all mysteries, yet it became openly revealed in Christ. The greatest of all mysteries is now identified with its subject, namely Christ the Messiah, the divine secret of all ages, the burden of all prophetic thought, the ultimate purpose of God's plan for the world: and this is none other than 'Christ in you' as you find your perfection and completion in Him. And this 'hope,' this spiritual ideal, can be realized only 'in Christ.' This divine power of Christ which became dynamic in Paul, showing what it can do in one human life, is meant to do the same in every man. 'It is no longer I that live, but Christ that liveth in me.'

CHAPTER II

PAUL'S GREAT COMMENDATION OF CHRISTIAN TRUTH

Analysis

Section 4. 2 $^{1-7}$.

Paul's concern for the Colossians and their neighbours.

Section 5. 2 $^{8-18}$.

Paul's polemic against the Judaeo-Gnostic philosophy at Colosse, directed—

(a) against its general principles as limiting the sufficiency of Christ and the Christian's completeness in Him; and—

Section 6. 2 $^{16-23}$.

(b) against the particular claims of the false teachers and the Jewish ritualistic observances, viz.:

(1) Legalism.
(2) Angel-worship.
(3) Asceticism.

Introduction

The actual statement of Paul's Christology is complete with the 23rd verse of Chapter I. Christ is the full revelation of the Infinite God: He is the climax of the whole evolutionary process in nature: He is the Head of that ideal Church which is the whole Cosmos conceived as the Body of God.

So far, however, all this is given in terms of metaphysical theory; and there is a wide gulf between metaphysical theory and personal religious experience. There is a microcosmos we call the human soul; and here, too, it is possible to find another dualism at work. Into this universe of the individual soul the Christ must come to make Himself the centre, drawing down all the fullness from God above, redeeming all that cries for redemption from beneath, so

making a 'temple of the Holy Ghost' which is in itself a world. It is
in order to make the transference from the metaphysical to the practical that the Apostle proceeds from the 24th verse of Chapter I,
and continues to the 17th verse of Chapter II. In other words, he
passes from the metaphysical to the personal. The proclamation of
the truth must be followed up by the commendation of the truth.
The responsibility of the teacher extends not merely to his orthodoxy
but also and especially to his ability to be convincing. Dogmatism
requires persuasion to make it acceptable and accepted. How is
Paul to express it so that those who were in danger of being 'earth-
quake-shocked' ($\mu\epsilon\tau\alpha\kappa\iota\nu o\hat{\upsilon}\mu\epsilon\nu o\iota$) may become 'firmly-grounded'
($\tau\epsilon\theta\epsilon\mu\epsilon\lambda\iota\omega\mu\acute{\epsilon}\nu o\iota$) and 'securely-builded' ($\acute{\epsilon}\delta\rho\hat{\alpha}\iota o\iota$) upon the hope
which they have personally heard, which has been heralded over
the Roman world, and of which the Apostle has himself become the
minister?

In the preceding chapter, by displaying the power and dignity of
Christ who offered His life as a sacrifice for the sins of the whole
world, and by teaching that God had in His everlasting mercy
appointed and accepted that sacrifice, Paul established the doctrine
of the Atonement on a sure foundation. 'Other foundation can
no man lay than that is laid.' By setting forth the extent and efficacy
of that Atonement, that through it even the Gentiles can now
rightly hope for a glorious resurrection, Paul presents the Gospel
to the Colossians to whom he propounds the way of salvation.
Consumed with the magnitude and eternal importance of this
essential doctrine, he begins the second chapter with a heightened
sense of urgency that the Colossians might understand why he was
sustaining such a combat of afflictions for preaching Christ as the
hope of glory to the Gentiles (verse 1).

His personal sufferings for that doctrine he ardently desired them
to know, that the hearts of the Gentiles might be uplifted by the
full assurance of its truth, for which he was ready to lay down his
life if only he could win them to an open profession of faith in
Christ as their redeemer. Paul has no hesitation in commending
his message by referring to the personal element in witness for
Christ. Much might be said of a right and wrong use of self-illustra-
tion: some fail by over-emphasis, others by lack of emphasis.
Young men newly ordained to the ministry need to be warned of a
wrong use of one's own individuality which can be quite blatant

and offensive; but there is also a proper use of the same which is the outward sign of the completest inward consecration. Where the end is Christ and not self, the Christian minister must be something more than a voice. All personal gifts, qualities, and graces are intended to be part of the servant's self-oblation. So it is in no spirit of self-esteem or self-advertisement that Paul refers to himself, to the effect that the passion of the teacher for his converts ought to count in the proclamation and recommendation of the Gospel of Christ Jesus. He points to a threefold claim which he is making upon the Colossians: he is sufferer, servant, and steward.

Having uncovered his burning heart to the readers of his Epistle, he proceeds with his polemic, or admonition, fully realising that it is the duty of the Christian teacher not merely to proclaim the truth of Christian doctrine nor merely to recommend it, but also to admonish by warning those who are in danger of error of the dire consequences. Had not the Galatians, with characteristic fickleness, yielded to the temptation to accept a 'different gospel' which was not 'another Gospel'? Although the situation in Colosse had not gone that far, as yet, the danger of heresy was obvious. Although Paul could still rejoice in the 'order' ($\tau \acute{a} \xi \iota s$) of the Colossian Church and its 'steadfastness' ($\sigma \tau \epsilon \rho \acute{\epsilon} \omega \mu a$)—both military virtues which Paul's association with the Praetorian Guard had taught him to appreciate— nevertheless he feels the need of warning them (with some mingling of metaphor) and would have them 'walk' in Christ, be 'rooted' in Christ, and be 'built up' in Christ, so that being well grounded in the faith they may stand unshaken before every shock that temptation may impose. And the particular temptation for the Colossians, though not like that which had already assailed the Galatians, namely, to hark back to the works of the Law as the best means of vindicating their righteousness in God's sight, but in the case of the Colossians to hark back to a formalism which sought spiritual perfection through the so-called discipline of asceticism and the consequent subjugation of the body. Both errors involved the choice of the imperfect instead of the complete. Beware of the Greek mystery religions! Beware of Judaizing legalism! Therefore, since the Gentiles entertained the highest veneration for the mysteries of their gods, Paul, in order to put a just value on the doctrines of the Gospel, calls the Atonement for the sins of the world, made by the sacrifice of Jesus, and the hope of pardon and a glorious resurrection to eternal life which the Gentiles could now entertain by virtue of that Atonement, 'the mystery of God and of Christ;' a mystery infinitely more wonderful, more profound, more certain than any of those so-called mysteries of the heathen deities of which the Phrygians were so very fond and by which they were so foolishly beguiled (verse 2).

Moreover, to show the Colossians that the things written in the preceding chapter (concerning Christ as the Image of the invisible God, and the Maker and Governor of all things) constitute the principal part of the mystery of God and Christ, Paul now re-introduces the subject by observing that in Christ 'are laid up all the treasures of Wisdom and Knowledge' (verse 3). This second reference to Christ's dignity was the more necessary because the false teachers at Colosse, endeavouring to discredit His mediation and gospel, affirmed that He was 'nothing but a man.' Accordingly they claimed a superior dignity and office for the Angels 'by whom the Law was given.' Paul's purpose was to prevent his Christians being deceived with 'enticing speeches' (verse 4). He goes on to assure them that his anxiety for the purity of their faith proceeded from his own profound concern for them and their highest interests (verse 5): and therefore he strives to persuade them that Christ is the Image of the Unseen God, the Maker and Governor of the universe, the Saviour of mankind, and the only Mediator between God and Man; and commands them to 'walk in Him', constantly holding fast to that belief and to yield Christ the honour and obedience due to His greatness and majesty (verse 6); and to continue ever closely united to Him, built upon Him, and established firmly in the faith of this true doctrine of the Christ; and to give thanks to God for the revelation vouchsafed to them (verse 7).

The Colossians, like many in our own time, sought to disguise the essential incompleteness of their views by the use of high-sounding terms. For the first and only time in all his writings, Paul introduces that much abused word *Philosophy*. As first used by Pythagoras it was a very modest term, implying a love of wisdom which, nevertheless, disclaimed the title of Wisdom itself. It was rather a longing to be wise. But no *philosophos* was prepared to describe himself as *sophos*. It was enough to be a searcher for truth. But the philosophy which was luring the Colossian Christians away from Christ was grossly pretentious and wholly inadequate. Its source 'is of men.' Its intrinsic character 'is of the world.' Its effect is not the freedom of mind and spirit, but a return to the bondage from which Christ had ransomed believers by His death. Paul exhorted them, therefore, to take care that no false teacher 'makes spoil of you' through the unsatisfactory and wholly unsatisfying philosophy of the Platonists which was calculated to support the heathen idolatry. The strong word translated 'maketh spoil of you' suggests the raid which the Gnostics believed Satan to have made into the realm of Light; or possibly, considering the Assyrian traditions of Tarsus, Paul was picturing to himself the long line of dejected captives who had in past ages suffered deportation at the cruel will of some Eastern tyrant. But by baptism those to whom Paul wrote had been redeemed and translated into the Kingdom of God's Son. Yet, with their own consent the 'evil power' had reclaimed them, and the self-deluded prisoners were passing ignominiously back to accept the yoke anew. With their faces turned towards the obsolete, they were walking not 'towards the sunrising' but into the twilight of the Old Testament dispensation, and seeking for angel and other mediators as of old. The result was bondage, indeed a bondage even more hopeless than the servitude to legalism which had been the bane of the Galatians.

Their error was both Theological and Practical; facts which require some elucidation:

(1) *The Theological error* consisted in substituting for the perfect mediatorship of Christ a whole series of figments created by men's imagination. This is set forth in four pregnant participial phrases, which may be summarized as follows:

(i) Worship of Angels, suggested by the fear of being judged presumptuous should one avail himself of the mediatorship of Christ, is a self-chosen (voluntary) and therefore false humility. In the face of the divine assurance of Fullness, this is the sin of sheer diffidence.

(ii) The consequence of this unworthy diffidence is that we take shelter in figments of our own invention. Experience shows that they who refuse to make their own the inheritance of Christ, invariably endeavour to find some lesser and easier way of meeting their spirit's need. The anxious *Ora pro nobis* addressed to the Blessed Virgin Mother, Queen of Heaven, or to the holy saints surrounding her, may quite unwittingly hide the choice of a lesser mediatorship which conceals the fear, begotten by lack of wholesome faith, of taking Christ at His word; and at the same time expressing a sub-merged doubt in the complete validity of the Incarnation as a means of reconciling man to God.

(iii) Next in order comes a kind of inevitable pride in our self-chosen limitation: an inflation with vanity and self-conceit which is a further affront to God. It is this obstinate maintenance of segmentary truth, which men wilfully substitute for 'the fullness,' that is the essence of modern Sectarianism. Perhaps men find it easier to cling with ill-founded assurance to their own self-selected fragment than to the great rock of Truth itself. They become so enclosed in their own arrogance that they are incapable of believing any point of view other than their own. In theological interpretation they are perfect virtuosi at exegetical evasion. This too is a sin against the Truth embodied, like the Love, in the Incarnation.

(iv) There is that which sums up the whole dreadful error, cause and consequence alike, namely, 'not holding the Head.' *Holding* (κρατῶν) rather than *having* (ἐχῶν), since to seize upon and retain hold of Christ in His proper relation to God and man is the secret of all security.

The heathen idolatry which was being clamped upon the Colossians was 'the worship of angels' as beings superior to Christ in knowledge and power; and was wholly contrary to the duty which they owed to Christ alone (verse 8) 'in whom dwelleth all the Fullness of the Godhead bodily' (verse 9). Thus, to be made complete in Christ, whether in knowledge or sanctification or pardon or favour with God, Christ's disciples need have no recourse to angels or the Mosaic law or Greek philosophy. In every respect they are 'made complete' by Him who is the Head of all government and power; the Head and Ruler of all angelic hosts (verse 10). In particular, Christ's disciples, by the 'circumcision not made with hands,' the Christian circumcision which consists of 'cutting out' the whole mass of 'sins of the flesh,' are far more effectually purified than by means of any Jewish rite or Pythagorean abstinence and mortification (verse 11). This 'Christian circumcision' was accomplished by their baptism in which their being 'buried beneath the water' typified the death and burial of their 'old man,' their unredeemed nature, through the death of Christ. Similarly, their emergence from the water of baptism was the emblem and pledge of their resurrection with Christ to eternal life, so that being pardoned by

Him they were also purified by Him and made 'complete' in Him, and therefore had no need of Levitical expiations (verses 12–13). And to show that by His own death Christ had made both Jew and Gentile complete in respect of pardon, Paul observed that Christ had blotted out the moral precepts of the law of nature as sanctioned in the Law of Moses with the curse.

(2) This brings us to the *Practical error* which springs from the misconception of theology.

The 'régime of ordinances'—'handle not, taste not, touch not'—will always possess a power of attractiveness to men, especially to reformers in a hurry. From the time of Constantine to the present day such a régime has appealed to many as the cure for every evil and the guarantee of every moral value. But, as Paul so splendidly puts it, there is in this method no such regenerative power as will exhaust the lusts of the flesh and make life spiritually constructive. Only the life of Christ, planted within, can give to both body and soul their true freedom; not, of course, that 'the law of Christ' is without obligations, but that the *compulsion to fulfil* these obligations, which develops as the 'fruit of the indwelling Spirit,' must be essentially different in character from the compulsion of the Law. The moral failure of Legalism, moreover, is paralleled by the moral failure of Asceticism. Again, experience proves that acts of asceticism can be entirely unrelated to morals.

But Paul is not content to point out the loss sustained by those who prefer the part to the whole, the imperfect rather than the perfect, incompleteness instead of 'the Fullness.' As in his letter to the Galatians, he makes the master-stroke of his argument the lifting up of the Cross of Christ and the re-affirmation of the significance of Christ's death and resurrection in their relation to the Incarnation.

'The handwriting of ordinances' was wholly disadvantageous to the Gentiles because it subjected them, as well as the Jews, to death for every offence; but Christ had erased that handwriting and in its blotted-out state had nailed it to His Cross in order to make all men realize that the Law, on account of its utter weakness, was abolished, and the curse with it (verse 14).

Furthermore, Christ's disciples are 'made complete' in respect of Governments, Powers, etc.; for such of the Angels as are inimical to mankind He has stripped of their power, and triumphed over them by His Cross. He has made a public exhibition of them. Therefore no one need be afraid when he recollects the malice and power of evil spirits, nor be tempted to worship them either from hope or fear (verse 15). Indeed, to return to the dispensation of the Principalities and Powers after experiencing the dispensation of Christ is not merely to go back, retreat, retard, but it is altogether to prove renegade and to repudiate Christ. Christ had died to render null and void the very 'philosophy' whose blandishments were proving so dangerously attractive to an ill-balanced and ill-established faith.

Two striking words are employed here by Paul, viz.: the *cheirograph* or 'note of hand' in verse 14, and *triumph* in verse 15.

(i) While the cheirograph, or bond, was outstanding against a man, the consequence was servitude. Just such a bond was the Old Testament law, standing against us in the three-fold character of standard, accuser, and avenger. In Roman Law, in order to cancel such a bond, it was usual to strike a nail through the document and tear it from top to bottom. This is precisely what Christ had done with the Old Testament law by dying; He had taken the indictment with Him upon the Cross and there by His absolute obedience unto death He had discharged it in full for all mankind. He cancelled it with the nails that rent the sacred body, and the torn fragments of the cancelled cheirograph were buried with the Saviour in His tomb. Indeed the very dynasty under which the document had been served on mankind has been for ever subverted by the death of Christ. In brief, the dispensation of the Law is over, and its writs no longer run.

(ii) Paul now passes to the second metaphor, viz: the *triumph*. This fifteenth verse is one of the most striking in the whole Epistle. The Revised Version has: 'having put off from Himself the principalities and powers,' a translation hard to justify. The Latin Fathers favour: 'having put off from Himself (His Body) He made a spectacle of the principalities and powers (as His captives).' This is supported by the R.V. margin. But the Greek Fathers seem to come nearer to a right understanding of the passage, as follows: 'Having despoiled the principalities and powers (i.e., having stripped them of their arms) He made of them a public show,'[1] just as a Roman conqueror, after triumphing over the foe, returned to Rome laden with the spoils of his victim, in order to make a public spectacle of the trophies won. So Christ, after having once for all

---

[1] But see my trans. of verse 15, and textual notes.

by His death subjugated the ancient world-rulers (κοσμοκράτορες) who had, as angels or as emanations, received the homage of men, now in His glorious triumph used the *feretrum* of the Cross to display before men's eyes the trophies of His redeeming love. All the armour of His rivals He has stripped away, and lo, He rides forth to reign for all eternity King of kings and Lord of lords.

The Apostle now proceeds from metaphysical theory to personal religion and gives the Colossians two exhortations founded on the doctrine laid down in verse 10, namely, (1) that since they were fully aware of their duty by the precepts of Christ, they were not to permit any Judaizing teacher to rule them concerning meats, drinks, festivals, new moons, or sabbaths (verse 16): these, even in the Mosaic dispensation, were of no value in themselves, but only as shadows of Gospel blessings. Consequently, as the body of which these services were the shadows was Christ's Body, the Church, and as all the blessings which they represented were now bestowed by Christ on His Church, there was no more need of the Mosaic shadows to prefigure them (verse 17). (2), that, since Christ was the Head of all government and power, the Colossians were not to permit any teacher tinctured with Platonic philosophy to cause them to lose their reward, namely, the benefit of Christ's mediation, by persuading them to worship Angels. These false teachers intruded into matters concerning the nature and office of angelic beings and astral powers of which they could not in the nature of things have any real knowledge at all (verse 18). In addition, these false teachers renounced Christ's authority over all government and powers. Yet, by His influence alone the Church would grow. By thus renouncing Him they deprived themselves of the benefit of His personal intercession as well as every other blessing which He had 'purchased for believers' (verse 19). The plain fact is that the Christian stands at the beginning of a new era inaugurated by Christ. What therefore is essential to every Christian is nothing less than the reproduction of the Christ-character in the life of every believer. To be a Christian is to be Christ-like. The baptism of the Christian is the pledge and the earnest of that reproduction. As for the whole human race the death and resurrection of Christ was the crossing of the dividing line which separates the New Order from the Old, so for the individual the sacrament of baptism is his translation out of the Kingdom of Darkness into the Kingdom of

Light, viz.: the Kingdom of the Son of God's Love. Baptism is therefore both death and resurrection in one sacramental rite; 'a death unto sin and a new birth unto righteousness.'

Having thus taught the Colossians their clear duty, Paul confronts them with searching questions: Since by your baptism, and by your very profession of the Christian faith, you have renounced your former religious and philosophical opinions in as far as they are contrary to Christ's Gospel, why have you subjected yourselves to the ordinances which are built upon them? (verse 20), namely, the Pythagorean precepts 'eat not, taste not, touch not' (verse 21) such meats as occasion the destruction of life in order that they may be so used; therefore partake in no way of animal food (verse 22)? These foolish precepts together with those of the Platonic philosophers regarding angelology have an 'appearance' of wisdom and logic since they recommend a worship voluntarily offered, together with a show of humility and the mortification of the body; but in reality these asceticisms are utter foolishness and illogicality, especially those which enjoin abstinence from animal food as a means of mortifying human passions, since they make no provision for the legitimate needs of the body which is as real a part of our nature as the soul, and needs to be nourished with such food and recreation as are fit for it. Otherwise the body cannot serve the soul in the functions and duties of daily life (verse 23).

Let us now consider all this, section by section.

SECTION 4.   PAUL'S CONCERN THAT MEN SHOULD KNOW THE TRUTH.
2 $^{1-7}$

Authorized Version	*Translation*
1 For I would that ye knew what great conflict I have for you, and *for* them at Laodicea, and *for* as many as have not seen my face in the flesh;	1 I want you to know what conflict I have endured for you as for them of Laodicea, and for all who have not seen me face to face:
2 That their hearts might be comforted, being knit together in love, and unto all riches of the full assurance of understanding, to the acknowledgement of the mystery of God, and of the Father, and of Christ;	2 that their hearts may be encouraged, that they may be drawn together in love, and that they may have all the riches of the full assurance of understanding, namely the full knowledge of this Mystery of God,
3 In whom are hid all the treasures of wisdom and knowledge.	3 in whom are all the treasures of wisdom and knowledge laid up.

G

4 And this I say, lest any man should beguile you with enticing words.

5 For though I be absent in the flesh, yet am I with you in the spirit, joying and beholding your order, and the stedfastness of your faith in Christ.

6 As ye have therefore received Christ Jesus the Lord, so walk ye in him:

7 Rooted and built up in him, and stablished in the faith, as ye have been taught, abounding therein with thanksgiving.

4 Now this I affirm in order that no one may deceive you with plausible arguments:

5 for although I am absent in the flesh, I am with you in spirit, rejoicing when I contemplate your order and the firmness of your faith in Christ.

6 Since, then, you have received Christ Jesus the Lord, walk in Him:

7 rooted in Him, built upon Him, and established in the faith, as you have been taught it, abounding with thanksgiving to God.

Exposition

Paul has striven to show both Jew and Gentile the way of their common salvation. The Church as Christ's Body is His continuing self upon earth in whose abiding presence and power all men are to be united as 'members one of another,' sharing in brotherhood the life of the Head. But for Paul there is nothing but suffering, striving, conflict, imprisonment at Caesarea and Rome. The inward wrestling which the Colossian heresy had occasioned in Paul's anxious mind had caused him much pain; and the heresy had now spread to Laodicea, and Paul is deeply concerned for this endangered Church. He appeals, therefore, to their hearts, the whole inner man as the vital centre of man's personality, that they may enjoy the wealth of sound conviction by a clear and sufficing assurance that the Gentiles are joint-partakers of God's promise in Christ. Although God's purpose in Christ, like the mystery of God's Love itself, is stupendous, it is not unintelligible. Here is a Mystery of infinitely more significance than any of the so-called Eleusinian mysteries. In God's mystery, namely Christ, are to be found all the treasures of wisdom and knowledge, and complete satisfaction for intellect and heart alike. The profoundest truths, the deepest realities, are to be discovered here. There are infinite treasures of Truth awaiting the inquiring man. The deeper he goes, the richer the treasure. 'Hidden' was a word beloved of the mystical Theosophists, and Paul is ever ready to use such words in his effort to show the true meaning consistent with his Christology. Even words need to be redeemed from wrong use and meaning. False reasoning always leads to wrong conclusions. Plausible arguments are calculated to persuade, but they may be wholly devoid of truth, despite their subtle appeal. But men can enter into the Christ-mystery which requires the venture of faith, less by a process of philosophical reasoning than by the clear guidance of the Holy Spirit, whose inspiring presence in heart and mind alike gives a clearer comprehension of divine truth than they could hope to achieve by logical processes of thought alone. Spiritual truth is spiritually discerned, oftener by a flash of inspiration than by any amount of scientific research. Faith in the Lordship of Christ is the rule that guides all conduct and tests all doctrine within the Church. It is also to be the final confession of a reconciled universe and a united humanity.

To 'walk in Christ' is to live as men mystically united with Him. He in us, and we in Him. It is not a so-called 'philosophy of life' men need, but a vital fellowship with the living Christ, a growing thing, nothing static, never standing still, but a development both purposeful and progressive, a systematically continued process that is always moving towards perfection, like a cathedral in process of building, 'built up from hour to hour in Him.' Faith is an active principle, living, dynamic, energizing the whole life and conduct that springs from it.

SECTION 5.   PAUL'S POLEMIC AGAINST THE JUDAEO-GNOSTIC PHILO-
SOPHY OF THE DAY. 2 8-15

Authorized Version

8 Beware lest any man spoil you through philosophy and vain deceit, after the tradition of men, after the rudiments of the world, and not after Christ.

9 For in him dwelleth all the fulness of the Godhead bodily.

10 And ye are complete in him, which is the head of all principality and power:

11 In whom also ye are circumcized with the circumcision made without hands, in putting off the body of the sins of the flesh by the circumcision of Christ:

Translation

8 Beware lest anyone makes spoil of you through philosophy and vain deceit, which is according to the tradition of men, according to the so-called Elements of the world, and not according to Christ:

9 For in Him dwells all the Fullness of the Godhead bodily,

10 and you are made complete in Him who is the Head of all government and power,

11 in whom also you have been circumcised with a circumcision made without hands, by the stripping off of the body of the flesh, in the circumcision of Christ,

12 Buried with him in baptism, wherein also ye are risen with *him* through the faith of the operation of God, who hath raised him from the dead.

12 being buried with Him in your baptism, in which you have been also raised with Him (reiterated in verse 13) through your faith in the mighty power of God who raised Him from the dead.

13 And you, being dead in your sins and the uncircumcision of your flesh, hath he quickened together with him, having forgiven you all trespasses;

13 For you who were dead by reason of your trespasses and the uncircumcision of your flesh, He has made alive together with Him, having forgiven us all our trespasses.

14 Blotting out the handwriting of ordinances that was against us, which was contrary to us, and took it out of the way, nailing it to his cross;

14 He has blotted out the handwriting of Ordinances (the whole rigmarole of 'regulations') concerning us, which was opposed to us, and has taken it away from us, nailing it to the Cross,

15 *And* having spoiled principalities and powers, he made a shew of them openly, triumphing over them in it.

15 having spoiled the demonic Principalities and Powers, He made a public show of them, triumphing over them by the Cross.

Exposition

Paul was too great a scholar to undervalue the importance of sound learning. He does not condemn the pursuit of true philosophy but the theosophical speculations of the day, which concerned themselves with such inanities as spirit-worship and the philosophical concepts of the Hellenists concerning 'daemons' (cf. 1 *Cor.* 10 [20]) or the supernatural agencies whom they represented as carrying men's prayers to God through a peculiar system of angelic beings who, according to Philo, are the 'presidents of the princes of the Almighty who, although He knows all things beforehand, finds it more expedient for us mortals to make use of such mediators, that we may the more admire and reverence the Supreme Governor, and the great power of His government.' Even in Tobit's day the mediation of angels was believed in by the Jews, for the angel who conducted Tobit said (12 [15]): 'I am Raphael, one of the seven holy angels which present the prayers of the saints.' The aim of the Alexandrian-Judaic school which had existed for two centuries at least, and had diffused its ideas far and wide, was to transform Judaism by interpreting it under philosophical principles, teaching that 'It is the philosophical man who holds converse with God.'

Paul warns the Church of the influence of such philosophy in corrupting the Gospel. These so-called 'principles' are nothing but the 'traditions of men,' mere 'rudiments,' crude beginnings, faulty and imperfect religious ideas, *elementa mundi* or the so-called 'powers of nature,' the 'heavenly bodies' or 'elemental spirits' worshipped as gods, and identified by the Jews as 'angels who are God's agents' in the direction of affairs in this world. Or again, Paul may mean those supposed 'unseen supernatural beings' who were thought to have malign influence over men; demonic agents and emissaries of the Evil One. But none of this is 'according to Christ': He is the norm and test of Truth. In Him are the abiding Realities, because in Him 'dwelleth all the Fullness of the Godhead bodily.' Paul here renews the warning which had been broken off at verse 4, and now returns to his doctrine of the Pleroma.

Here, then, is the supreme significance of Christ. Eternal love has made itself incarnate, visible, tangible, in the Person of Jesus Christ. Neither God nor Jesus could be 'explained' without recognition of this compelling fact. God and Christ are One, not merely 'at one' in mind and purpose, but essentially One in nature and eternal Being. Jesus is the Pleroma of God's wisdom, love, power, in every aspect of divinity which, in Christ, is full, perfect, complete, absolute. All that God is, Christ is, without difference or inequality. The undivided Pleroma of I [19] now reveals its twofold nature—it is 'the Fullness of the Godhead,' and yet it 'dwells corporeally in Christ.' All that is in God's nature is fully present in Christ. The fullness of Perfection essential to God is necessarily essential to Christ. It is the whole Divine Nature which by the Incarnation belongs to the man Christ Jesus by virtue of the union of the Divine nature with the human in His Person. Christ is 'of One Substance with the Father.'

Paul's teaching is the negation of the philosophy of the day with its mediating angels and clouds of spiritual emanations, and contempt of the body and the natural world. With Paul the body is 'the temple of the Holy Ghost.' Although 'pleroma' was a Gnostic term, the 'Fullness' was *Christ*, and all that concerns the body must be seen as wholly Christian.

It is the 'complete' Christ who alone can make us complete. His *pleroma* is our *plerosis*. There is no need to turn elsewhere for spiritual blessedness or final salvation, either for individual Christians or the Church as a whole. Paul shows the absurdity of adding either the so-called doctrines or the traditions of men to the Gospel, for if Christians are 'made complete' in Christ in sanctification, pardon, and protection, then all human additions to the Gospel are a serious corruption of it, and must be rejected outright. Christ is all-sufficient for everyman. He is the Head of all government and power. He is Head in the whole cosmic sense. This is the doctrine that affords the profoundest consolation to the people of God, for it assures them that nothing befalls them without His knowledge, and that 'all things' will, in the end, according to His purpose, work together for their good. Therefore, since Christ is the Maker and Lord of all power, visible and invisible, including every so-called 'angelic power' with its magical efficacy or astral phenomenon, we Christians are 'in Him,' and therefore under no constraint to look to 'philosophy so-called' for our salvation which comes from Him alone. And this includes such 'commandments of men' as the old traditional rite of Circumcision which was not only insisted upon by the Judaizers as a matter of Law and obligation, but by the new philosophical teachers as essential to spiritual completeness, and as a symbolic moral efficiency—'the excision of all the pleasures and passions, and the destruction of impious opinion' (Philo: *Treatise on Circumcision*). For Paul, however, Baptism is the Christian circumcision, the new symbolic expression of the *moral change* which both Paul and his opponents considered necessary, although they saw it in different senses. Baptism is a real sanctification which renders men more acceptable to God than either Jewish circumcision or the mortifications prescribed by Pythagorean philosophy. 'They that are Christ's have crucified the flesh with its affections and lusts.' The organic life of the body is delivered from the dominion of sin which makes the body its instrument. Christian baptism has thus two implications: (i) of dying to the old order, and (ii) of rising to the new life: 'being buried with Him in your baptism' and 'raised with Him in His resurrection.' Here is a phrase which puts the reality of 'the death to sin' beyond dispute. Thus 'having been buried' is now replaced in the antithesis by the more assertive 'You were raised.' 'Dead unto sin, and alive unto God,' is one indivisible experience.

Throughout the whole of Paul's religion there reverberates, like the stroke of a great cathedral bell, 'Christ is risen! alive for evermore!'; and it is in the Risen Christ that the Christian finds all the assurance he needs for life in this present world. Trial may come, tribulation may come, even death itself may come, but the Christian knows that 'death is swallowed up in victory!' He begins *now* to live *eternally*, because his life 'is hid with Christ in God.' The Resurrection is fundamental to the Christian Faith, for without the resurrection the death of Christ on the Cross would have been powerless to save; and without a risen, living, present Christ, with whom through faith the believer can come into union, all the benefits of Christ crucified would have had to stand unappropriated for ever. Indeed, the resurrection proves the Lordship of Christ over life and death. His transcendent Personality could never have impressed His disciples, however great His spiritual stature, as did His resurrection. The ideal of the Creation had been attained. Unless we are to regard the Creation as having no ultimate meaning for the Personality that crowns it, and no lasting value for the Creator Himself, we must believe that those in whom the true life has been realized (even if only as yet in principle) do not only survive death, but find the fullness and fruition of their life in God. To disbelieve this is to fail utterly of belief in God.

If the true life of man is, as the Christian religion holds, life in union with God, it cannot but be Eternal, and, according to its measure in man, enter into the 'glory' which belongs to the Divine Life distinctively. It is even *now* Eternal Life, and all who are united to Christ are already 'made alive with Him' in a life over which death has no ultimate power at all.

It must never be forgotten that the Resurrection was the creative energy out of which Christendom was born. It was the risen and exalted Christ that was preached to the world: it was in Him that men were asked to believe: to Him they were to look for salvation; and if there had been no reality in it, proved by experience, how long would Christianity have continued to exist? Men were convinced by personal experience that they were indeed living in vital union with a living Lord. He was a real Presence with them. He was their very life, dwelling in the heart through faith. 'Christ in them' provided that precise union in which they were conscious of being raised into the sphere of the Divine and Eternal. 'For since by man—Adam the Failure—came death, by man—Christ the Triumphant—came also the resurrection of the dead: for as in Adam all die, even so in Christ shall all be made alive.' Sin reduces all men to the same level: redemption lifts them

together to God's new plane. 'The handwriting of Ordinances' had
been 'blotted out.' Jesus 'nailed it to the Cross.' This is of such
extreme importance in Paul's thought that we must pause here for a
careful examination of his thesis.

AN EXAMINATION OF PAUL'S REFERENCES TO THE LAW, THE REMISSION OF SINS, AND THE CROSS

(i) The first result of Christ's crucifixion to Paul's thought seems
to be that, by it, for the Christian, the Law was abrogated. This
was an event which could not have been foreseen. No more
devoted servant of Judaism ever lived than he; but now he accepted
Christ as Messiah and Saviour. For so doing, the Law pronounced
him anathema. He accepted the judgement; but to his surprise he
found that as an exile from Judaism he entered the land of blessedness and liberty, the possibility of which he had never dreamed.
But the impossible had become the actual.

Paul *as a Jew* regarded the Law as divinely appointed. Even in
the great change of his faith he never lost this sense of the divine
origin of the Law; only his relation to it *as a Christian* involved
consequences previously unsuspected. Now he found in the Law
itself utterances which implied that from the beginning it was
meant to be transitory. Thus he passed out from under the Law as
reverently as he had previously lived under it. It was through the
Law itself that he died to the Law. No other power than that of
the Law could have released him from its authority.

(ii) The second result of the crucifixion, one that was involved
in the one just stated, was the remission of sins that had been committed against the Law, and the removal of the condemnation which
these sins had incurred. When the Jewish Law was abrogated, old
scores were wiped out, and old offences lost their condemnation;
just as in the time of the French Revolution, when the tyranny under
which France had grievously suffered was overthrown, the prisoners
that were languishing under its condemnation for crimes committed
against it came forth into the light of liberty. So now, the penalties
of the Law were no longer dreaded, for the Law that had imposed
them had ceased to be.

Now all this, it will be observed, is quite contrary to the generally
accepted view of Paul's teaching. The customary doctrine is that
Christ by His death bore the penalty of all human transgression;

that the sins of those who trusted in Him were thus remitted; and that, on account of this, in some way which it seemed utterly impossible to discover, the Law was abrogated. But between these two transactions, (i) the remission of sins, and (ii) the abrogation of the Law, there was no clear, logical connection.

The view which I am now expressing reverses the process. *The Law itself was FIRST abrogated*, and through this abrogation of the Law, the sins which had been committed under it were remitted. This makes the connection between the two transactions both logical and inevitable.

Do I find any support for this view in Paul's own doctrine? I suggest that Paul's Epistle to the Colossians gives the fundamental answer: 'And you, being dead through your trespasses and the uncircumcision of your flesh, you, I say, did He quicken together with Him, having forgiven us all our trespasses; *having blotted out (cancelled) the bond* written in ordinances that was against us, which was contrary to us: and He hath taken it out of the way, nailing it to the Cross' (2 13-14). Here we are clearly told that our trespasses are forgiven, because the bond that was against us by its ordinances, was taken out of the way. This refers unmistakably to the Jewish Law. Therefore it was *the Law that was nailed to the Cross*. In other words, the Law and Christ came into collision. The Law condemned Him, and won a temporary victory; but in condemning Him it condemned itself absolutely. By this last exercise of authority it abdicated its authority. Having crucified the Lord of glory, it crucified itself with Him. Thus it was nailed to the Cross by a permanent crucifixion. Christ rose glorified: the Law died eternally. The evil bondage was lifted for ever from humanity's heart. The curse was dead. The Law was ended. Seen thus, the dialectic of Paul, by which the Law was the agent of its own overthrow, is quite amazing. If this were a bit of legal strategy we could not fail to admire its audacity; but it is the more admirable when we see it in the natural working of a philosophical mind which, by its very reverence for the Law, was emancipated from the Law. Certainly it is not too much to claim that it was Paul's dialectic which transferred the teaching of Jesus without substantial change from what threatened to be local to world-wide influence, setting it free from local forms of thought so that it could appeal to the universal consciousness of mankind. This Pauline passage (2 13, 14, 15) insists that the forgiveness of our trespasses was the result of this 'crucifixion of the Law,' i.e., of its abrogation through the crucifixion of Christ. The generally accepted view makes the forgiveness primary and the abolition of the Law secondary; while, as I see it, Paul's letter to the Colossians makes the abolition of the Law primary and the forgiveness secondary. In this connection it is important to notice that the passage which begins with the forgiveness of sins, basing this upon the abrogation of the Law, passes at once to the exhortation to the maintenance of Christian liberty: 'Let no man therefore judge you in meat, or in drink, or in respect of a feast day or a new moon or a sabbath day' (2 ¹⁶). The Christian is Christ's freeman: let him not return to the old bondage.

But what can this have to do with the remission of sins? I suggest we have here a logical consistency which brings order and sequence into the Pauline thesis in cases where they seem most lacking. If, however, this explanation of Paul's doctrine of the remission of sins by the death of Christ, namely, that all our sins were remitted because the Law was now done away, seems too indirect and cold, I will call attention to the fact that it is most powerfully suggested in the most impassioned utterance of Paul that has come down to us: 'O death, where is thy sting? O grave, where is thy victory? The sting of death is sin; and the power of sin is the Law. But thanks be to God who giveth us the victory through our Lord Jesus Christ' (1 *Cor.* 15 ⁵⁵⁻⁵⁷). In this passage, the idea that the power of sin is lost because the Law is done away fits perfectly with the passion of the outburst; while the explanation generally given, that the Law loses its power because in the substitutionary death of Christ its terrible demands were met and an angry God placated, seems both awkward, far fetched, and altogether contrary to what we believe of the Father of our Lord Jesus Christ.

SALVATION FOR THE GENTILES. The question now presses: What part had the Gentiles in all this? How could the death of Jesus be in any sense regarded as the propitiation of their sins when, being wholly outside the Jewish Law, they had not sinned against it?

Although the Gentile was not 'under the Law,' he was, as Paul insists, a sinner (*Rom.* 1 ¹⁸⁻³²) because he had a conscience, and conscience taught him the law of God (*Rom.* 2 ¹⁴ᶠᶠ). Man's guilt has become his fate. Sin controls him until it finally destroys him.

'The sting of death is sin, and the strength of sin is the law' (1 *Cor.* 15 [56]). As Dr. Bultmann has said: 'The law, which is intrinsically holy, righteous and good, and comes from God, becomes a lethal power.'[1] To the Jew, the Law, given by Moses, was the vehicle of a promise in which the Gentile had no part, and therefore for him there was no hope. But when the Law was annulled, the promise which it contained remained in its fullness and for the first time appeared in its true significance: the limitation which had excluded the Gentile from 'the hope of Israel' was done away. Christ was the universal Christ in whom there was neither Jew nor Gentile. The most luminous passage which clarifies the whole subject is contained in Ephesians 2 [11-22]:

> Remember, then, that as far as race is concerned, you are Gentiles, called by that opprobrious epithet 'The Uncircumcized' by those who call themselves 'The circumcized' because, being Jews, they underwent a surgical operation. Thus there was no Christ for you: you were outlaws from the commonwealth of Israel and foreigners to the promise under the Covenant. You were without God and had nothing to hope for in the world. But now you are in Christ Jesus: now, through the blood of Jesus, you have been brought close, you who were once so far away. He is our bond of peace; our bond, because He has made the two nations one, breaking down the dividing wall that was a barrier between us. He has abrogated the Law with all its detailed regulations, and has made our two races one in Himself. Out of two distinct individuals He has, so to speak, by uniting both in Himself, created one new man. Thus He has established peace and ended the old hostility by reconciling both to God through the offering of His own body on the cross. So He came, and His message was a proclamation of peace for you who were far off as also for those who were more closely related to Himself. Being united in the same Spirit, we both alike have free access through Him to the Father. Thus you are no longer exiles, nor licensed aliens: indeed you now enjoy rights of equal citizenship with the Brethren and the members of God's own household. You are part of that one building whose foundation consists of the Apostles and Prophets and whose keystone is Jesus Christ Himself. In Him the whole fabric is bound together as each constituent part makes its own contribution to the completion of a holy temple dedicated to the Lord. In Him you Gentiles are being built in with the rest, so that God may find in you a dwelling place for His spirit.

Thus we see that the central thought is that Christ abolished the Law which had created the long-standing enmity between Jew and Gentile. Each had become a 'new man,' starting afresh, freed from the old condemnation, and ready for 'the new life' which came through Christ. Life was henceforth to be based not on external authority,

---

[1] Bultmann: *Primitive Christianity*, p. 192.

but upon the devotion of a heart transformed by the power of the living Christ through the indwelling of the Holy Ghost. Christ had struck off the chains from the human spirit. The Gospel of the Cross is the gospel of Freedom, not 'of Law' but 'in Love.'

This brings us to what may be called the second most important aspect of the gospel of Reconciliation. First, we saw that the idea of Reconciliation with God concerned the whole order of the universe. It is the act of God in reconciling 'the world' to Himself which gives us a universal Gospel, and opens the door of access to God for every sinner, Greek, Barbarian, Jew. But it goes further. As part of the universal Reconciliation, it includes, secondly, that of man to man, and implies the restoration of *unity* to humanity. The Cross becomes the means of unity and the source of peace, not only as between man and God, but as between man and man. The result was seen in the formation of the Christian Church wherein Jew and Gentile now met in brotherly fellowship on equal terms. None the less, there is a far wider application in respect of which it has been as yet imperfectly realized. We Christians, like all others, have failed to make actual in fact that which was made potential for all in Christ. We have not given due prominence to the fact that *the Cross* represents not only the Atonement of men to God, but of *man to man*. We have given too exclusively an individualistic application to that which is designed to bring about the actual and practical unity to mankind, to 'make peace' everywhere amongst men, to create 'one new man,' or collectively viewed, *one true family of God on earth.*

Because of this tragic failure the nations continue, despite all their Calvaries, to arm themselves against 'possible enemies' in the perfecting of instruments of mass destruction, whilst others grade their peoples into 'white and non-white,' thus repudiating the whole truth of the Christian Gospel as the Religion of Love. We forget that we cannot be at one with God while we continue to be at war with one another.

The same principle applies in its measure to industrial strife, the continual enmity between Capital and Labour, the Government and those who boast of their 'bargaining power' which becomes so menacing, and on occasion morally reprehensible. It is not unchristian for men to seek the way of equity or to cling to human rights, any more than it would be Christian for oppression or injus-

16834

tice to hold sway. But if right and justice are to prevail anywhere at all, then the Spirit of Christ must rule in men's hearts: on *both* sides His divine influence must be operative before which the spirit of strife may be banished and the things that are just and equal and all that makes for peace be found, established, and settled. It is the right spirit that is wanted to make things right. In no other way can men be brought into unity with God and one another. It is only Christ's spirit of sacrificial Love in human hearts that can ever bring about the true 'brotherhood of man.' And it is for the Christian Church, which exists for the furtherance of that Gospel, to take up with fresh endeavour and deeper consecration this *manward* bearing of the Divine purpose, both as concerning international disputes and all the various causes of dispeace in society. What Paul rightly described as 'demonic Principalities and Powers' from which Christ on the Cross delivered the world, are ever ready to lift their heads again in order to nullify man's redemption and bring him 'under the curse' once more, against which all his strivings will be unavailing. Not for the first time in human history have men mistaken Evil Powers for angelic theophanies, and thereby have brought themselves into appalling bondage and corruption.

SECTION 6. PAUL'S POLEMIC AGAINST PARTICULAR RELIGIOUS PRACTICES ARISING OUT OF FALSE PHILOSOPHY AND JEWISH RITUALISM

(1) LEGALISM. (2) ANGEL-WORSHIP. (3) ASCETICISM (2 $^{16-23}$).

Authorized Version

16 Let no man therefore judge you in meat, or in drink, or in respect of an holyday, or of the new moon, or of the sabbath *days*:

17 Which are a shadow of things to come; but the body *is* of Christ.

18 Let no man beguile you of your reward in a voluntary humility and worshipping of angels, intruding into those things which he hath not seen, vainly puffed up by his fleshly mind.

Translation

16 Therefore let nobody judge you in reference to meat, drink, festival, new moons or Sabbaths:

17 which are a shadow of things to come: but the body is Christ's Body.

18 Let no one rob you of your reward, by taking pleasure in false humility and angel-worship, meddling with things which he claims to have seen, vainly—being puffed up by his own carnal mind,

19 And not holding the Head, from which all the body by joints and bands having nourishment ministered, and knit together, increaseth with the increase of God.

20 Wherefore if ye be dead with Christ from the rudiments of the world, why, as though living in the world, are ye subject to ordinances,

21 (Touch not; taste not; handle not;

22 Which all are to perish with the using;) after the commandments and doctrines of men?

23 Which things have indeed a shew of wisdom in will worship, and humility, and neglecting of the body; not in any honour to the satisfying of the flesh.

19 and not holding firmly to the one Head by whom the whole body, through the joints and ligaments being supplied and compacted, increases with the increase of God.

20 Since you have died with Christ to the Elements of the world, why, as living in the world, do you subject yourselves to Ordinances?—

21 'Eat not! Taste not! Touch not!'—

22 all things that perish in the using; according to the commandments and doctrines of men—

23 which precepts have an appearance of 'wisdom,' by will-worship and humility and a not-sparing of the body; but are absolutely useless in combating the indulgence of our lower nature.

Exposition

Paul, having struck at the heart of a corrupting heresy now strikes at the characteristics which reveal themselves in practice. He insists upon Christian freedom from all merely human ordinances, even from those contained in a Law believed to be divine in its origin. Men who are complete in Christ, through His Cross and Passion, are under no obligation to obey either Pagan teachers or Judaizing proselytizers when they enjoin the Mosaic rites, the worship of angels, or bodily mortifications as the means of salvation. Paul's thesis is: Away with all this unreality and pedantry of dogmatic legalism together with all the contemptuous exclusiveness which claims a monopoly of all the vested rights in God. Refuse to be ruled by traditions which cannot of themselves achieve holiness of life. The private authority of the Ascetic Party which is already forming itself within the Church has no authority from Christ. The Levitical Law, the Nazaritic rites of the Essenes, the philosophizing Judaists, the so-called 'established customs which divine men have instituted' and which are held to be equally binding upon men, have all been abrogated by Christ. These so-called 'regulations' merely shadowed forth prophetically the coming Christian revelation and were thereby displaced for ever:

the shadow may belong to them, but the substance belongs to Christ. In Him we find the reality of which all the 'sacred ordinances' were but an anticipation. Do not allow yourselves to be defrauded of your prize by humility-exercises. Humility indeed! While the so-called 'philosopher' dotes on his 'visions' and claims to be exalted by his reasoning faculty by which he has penetrated into the secrets of the spiritual world and enjoys intercourse with angelic hosts, the plain fact is that his vaunted revelations and high flying Theosophy are nothing but the emanations of his own carnal mind with its natural inability to comprehend the spiritual life. These spiritualistic revelations of the invisible world are not to be mistaken for the Mysticism of the true Mystics who have so profoundly adorned and influenced the Christian Church throughout the Christian ages. It is only the truly spiritual mind that can apprehend God; and Paul does not try to define it: instead he gives the only true example, namely 'the mind of Christ.'

Paul here gives a warning against all theosophical and spiritualistic dreamery, and to beware of all refinements of Christianity which have the slightest tendency to derogate from the authority and honour of Christ who is both Head of the Church as of all existence. Disloyalty to the Head works its own destruction to 'the whole body' and disintegrates it. By the organic co-operation of the whole structure ('joints and ligaments being supplied and compacted') can the Body of Christ, the Church, be 'furnished with its supplies,' and enabled to receive and dispense to each single member the needful sustenance, thus adding to its divine growth.

Never did the Church need to give heed as now to this warning, when the 'rudimentary crudities' of newly-invented ideologies are striving to capture the human mind. They fought against Christ. They fought against Paul. But both Christ and Paul knew that human redemption was not to be won by fighting against the evil powers outside of man, but from man's *sinful self*. We hear much to-day of Human Freedoms—freedoms from war, from want, from fear; and great is the need for each and all of them. But the one dominating freedom which the world so desperately needs is freedom from sin. And that is something that must happen in the experience of every man if our modern world is to be saved from war and want and fear. All else is but a worthless substitute for 'the law of the spirit of life in Christ.' Man-made 'religion' is not the same as the religion of the man-in-Christ. The latter is not under bondage to heretics. Nor is he the sport of that interminable 'Quest for Truth' which earnestly seeks yet so tragically fails to find.

CHAPTER III

PAUL'S PRACTICAL APPLICATION : THE NEW LIFE IN CHRIST

Analysis

Section 7. 3^{1-17}

Paul passes from negative warnings to positive injunctions concerning the true Christian life and its practice, as contrasted with the false asceticism and visionary illusions of theosophy.

Section 8. $3^{18}-4^{1}$

Paul emphasizes the practicalities of Christian obligations in all the common relationships of family daily life.

Introduction

Paul avoided the error, which assails not a few scholars, of substituting academic theology for practical religion: he realized that both are necessary and that they must coalesce. In verse 12 of the preceding chapter he had made it plain to the Colossians that by their baptism they had been buried with Christ as dead persons in token of their having relinquished their former principles and practices, and also that they had been raised out of the water with Christ as an emblem and pledge of their resurrection with Him to eternal life. The former of these doctrines the Apostle had applied (2^{20}) to show the Colossians the absurdity of allowing themselves to be subjected to the old ritual precepts from which they had been freed by their death with Christ. And now, in his application of the latter doctrine, he tells them that since they had been raised with Christ out of the water of baptism and had thereby openly professed their hope of everlasting life, they were bound to do their utmost, by faith and holiness, expressed in daily living, to obtain full possession of the joys of heaven where Christ now reigns at God's right hand, vested with full power to bestow such joys on all who were able to receive them (verse 1). In particular, they were to set their hearts on 'things above,' and not on the riches and pleasures of this worldly world (verse 2). The more so, since, according to the present course of things, they were in great danger of being put to death by their persecutors for their faith, and of losing every earthly enjoyment. Or at any rate, they were sure to die at length. Yet the fear of death was not to disquiet them. Their bodily life being entrusted to Christ will be restored at the resurrection; so that when He comes to raise the dead and judge the world they too will appear with Him in glorified immortal bodies, and be put in possession of heaven's unspeakable joys (verse 4). In order that they might be capable of this great felicity, Paul exhorts them to mortify themselves, not after the Pythagorean manner, but by 'putting off' their inordinate carnality, fornication, etc. (verse 5).

Never since Paul's time has this doctrine needed more emphasis than now. We human beings are the inhabitants of two spheres—body and soul. Christ is Lord of both, as seen in the Incarnation and the Resurrection. One reason, perhaps the most dominating, for the growing immoralities of modern times, is the complete disregard of Christian teaching concerning the bodily life of man and woman, namely, that 'the body is the Temple of the Holy Spirit.' If this modern peril is not to overpower us as it overpowered Rome to her destruction, the Church must strive the harder for a great recovery of Christian sacredness in sex relations, not in the spirit of 'safety first' but of sanctity all the time. When the old world-order broke up, and the fall of the Roman Empire shook the foundations of the universe, there was a Christendom strong enough to play the essential part in the enormous task of reconstruction. Its strength was derived from its moral principles, and expressed in the daily life and conduct of humble men and women whose souls were 'daily renewed' by an indwelling Power that was not of themselves but of the Living Christ. They were 'strengthened with power through God's spirit in the inner man.' In Plutarch's heroes the *human* element of strength is supreme: in the biographies of the saints it is the *divine* element of spiritual and moral power flowing from vital contact with the Eternal Creator Spirit, a power unknown to the Greeks and Romans, producing a 'new creation' of men and women who seemed to belong to a different species and another world. This at least is clear: it is not natural decision or force of character that makes men and women conquerors over sin and death and time: it is a *new* force, expressing itself in unfashionable faith, in thought, purpose, and action, in speech, suffering, and sacrificial love; and this is the work of Him from whom all forms of energy proceed, but whose principal work in this universe is the creation of a special kind of character through which His kingdom will come on earth and His will be done for all mankind.

What Paul is here pleading for is that 'daily renewing'[1] which is the constant extension of Christian baptism until regeneration is complete. So life becomes a daily baptism, with a daily dying and a daily rising from the dead, a daily cleansing and a daily quickening, a daily putting off, and a daily putting on. This daily 'putting off' and 'putting on' are described in two paragraphs, 3 $^{5-11}$ and 3 $^{12-14}$. The putting off is a daily series of 'slayings' ($\nu\epsilon\kappa\rho\acute{\omega}\sigma\alpha\tau\epsilon$). It is also a discarding of those 'garments' which correspond to what Paul calls in his Epistle to the Galatians 'the works of the flesh.' These must be 'stripped off' before the believer can be admitted to the glad festival of the sons of God. Thus Paul tells the Colossians that however pleasing these abominations might be to heathen gods, they could only provoke the wrath of the one true God upon those who were guilty of such gross evil (verse 6); and that, though formerly, whilst they were heathens themselves, they lived in the habitual practice of these appalling vices (verse 7), it now became them in their Christian state to put them all away, together with fornication and every other form of wrong (verse 8), because at their baptism they professed to 'put off the old man with his carnal deeds' (verse 9).

Then comes the 'putting on.' Paul had written to the Ephesians of putting on armour. Here he speaks of the ordinary clothing of Christian virtue, with love as the 'girdle' which holds all together. In such a life of happy freedom, the festal freedom of a new order, is to be realized that which breaks down every barrier of condition and race, which shall make possible every social reform, and which shall ensure the final victory of Light over all the powers of Darkness. So the Colossians are to 'put on the new man' who is made through knowledge of the truth, after the image of God (verse 10). And to encourage them to acquire this new nature, he told them that it communicates such a dignity to him who possesses it that God does not regard the ordinary differences of race and language, Greek, Jew, etc., but that in this 'new creation' every man is honour-

[1] Cf. the Collect for Christmas Day, and Lent II.

able everywhere according to the degree in which he possesses this new nature, the nature of Christ (verse 11). Withal, to show them the splendour of the 'new man,' he describes his qualities: 'Bowels of mercies,' etc.; and urges the Colossians as 'the elect of God' to put them on (verses 12-13); and above all to put on love, which, as we observed, he represents as a girdle which completes and perfects the spiritual dress (verse 14).

The chapter opens with the claim that a Christocentric macrocosm must be reproduced as a Christocentric microcosm in the individual life. The vindication of this claim is supplied in the three concluding admonitions which close the section, namely, verses 15, 16, 17.

Thus, verse 15. Christ must be the *centripetal force* of personal religion. The peace of Christ must be 'umpire' or arbiter to pull all the contending forces of life together. To the Philippians he had written of the 'peace of God' as the 'garrison power' which, like the castle-keep, was to hold life safe. Here, using the term 'peace of Christ' (which some copyists found so unusual that they set it aside as impossible), he offers Christ's peace as reconciliation.

Verse 16—Because the worshippers of Cybele and Bacchus feigned themselves to be inspired by these idols, running through the streets and fields, in high frenzy, committing numberless extravagancies and singing bawdy songs in honour of the gods whom they worshipped, Paul sought to prevent the Colossians from joining in these madnesses, and commanded them to have the word of Christ dwelling in them richly, keeping it in remembrance and speaking of it with reverence; and in their social gatherings when they felt themselves moved by the spirit, instead of singing heathen songs to sing psalms and hymns and odes dictated by the Holy Spirit, all with sincere devotion to the honour of their Lord. In other words, Christ must also be the *centrifugal force* of life through which all the rich results of an 'indwelling Christ' may flow forth to the whole circuit of experience. The seeker after wisdom may tire himself out in the pursuit of philosophies which prove to be only flying goals, if not mirages. The indwelling Christ gives the true wisdom.

Verse 17—Because the heathen offered solemn thanksgivings to Bacchus as the giver of all good things mankind enjoys, Paul ordered the Colossians to ascribe all honour and praise to God alone, who is the real Author of every true and perfect gift; and to thank Him through the mediation of Christ. Christ must also be the *centre itself*, providing from thence the one motive for whatsoever is accomplished in thought, word, and deed. With any other centre all life goes necessarily awry: only the Christ-centred life is for ever secure from every evil assault.

Having thus far directed the Colossians, Paul concludes this chapter on the important note concerning the relative and social duties of life; that in their behaviour as citizens the Christians ought to be as distinguishable from the heathen as they were in their knowledge of true religion; all of which concerned such important issues as the duties of husbands and wives (verses 20-21); slaves (verses 22-25); and, last of all, masters and servants (4 ¹) with which Chapter III should properly have ended.

But what have these minor matters to do with the Cosmic Christ? Many commentators have expressed surprise at the sudden descent of the Apostle from the high level of academic argument so nobly sustained until we come to this concluding section which commences at 3 ¹⁸; and not a few notable scholars have held the view that, to all intents and purposes, Paul's great message was now complete, and that his intention was merely to add a few practical admonitions of a general character, and then conclude with the necessary personal greetings. Is this conception of the Epistle correct? Has the Pauline fire died down upon the altar? Has he descended from the sublime height of his great thesis on the absolute supremacy of Christ to offer merely a few simple and homely recommendations, in which some have detected the spirit of a reactionary respecting the relative duties of family life, etc., all of which have the appearance of mere trivialities after so profound a theme?

The answer surely is that religion is never quite so profound as when it is profoundly practical. Christ's work of Reconciliation must be continued throughout the world; reconciliation between Christians, within the family circle, within the local congregation, within nations, within every sphere of human injustice which the Christian conscience cannot go on tolerating. It was a matter of vital importance for Paul's readers to understand that the argument of the earlier sections of the Epistle leads inescapably to the practicalities which every Christian has to face in everyday life. It is not for highbrow philosophers, nor for thoughtless dilettanti that the

Apostle writes, but for men and women, struggling Christians, in every condition of life. Indeed the one object for which Truth is made plain, and the errors denounced which obscure it, is that Truth may be set free from the bonds of theory to work in the human world for the redemption of society. And here comes the test: if Truth is to succeed anywhere, here is the arena for the battle. Will it serve? Both here and in the Epistle to the Ephesians where Paul makes a similar and strikingly practical use of his highly intellectual Christological doctrine, the application is offered to ordinary men and women in 'the trivial round and common task' where religion so often perishes in the fight; to husbands, wives, fathers, children, masters, servants.

It must be remembered that at least one lamentable consequence of the ascetic turn which the Colossian heresy had taken was that men were disposed to connect the rejection of the domestic ties with a higher degree of spirituality. The very name *religious* was already beginning to be limited to those who practised religion apart from the normal obligations of society. The Pharisee was the privileged keeper of the Law, and therefore 'holy': the Publican, lacking leisure for the requisite scrupulosities, was 'accursed.' St. Simon Stylites wins the worship of the crowd, while the little lad who trudges across the burning sands to bring food and water to the holy man is not technically religious at all. Again, there was prevalent the disposition on the part of those who followed esoteric teachings to become impatient with the restraints of commonplace domestic morality. In the Early Church, in this very region of Phrygia, great scandal was caused by this wanton contempt for the ordinary conventions concerning sex-relations; contempt which led occasionally to outbreaks of most disgraceful license. Read the fourth century story of Glycerius the Deacon,[1] which shows how easily a fancied superiority to the common rule of decency can end in disastrous moral collapse. It is fitting, therefore, that the Apostle should show that the manifestation of the *Pleroma* is for the purpose of transfiguring the most common, even the most humdrum aspects of human life; a lesson which is needed quite as much to-day as then, for there are still in our midst those who walk with heads high in the air while their shoes are clogged with miry clay.

But there is yet another reason for this rallying to the support of a

[1] See Ramsay: *Church in the Roman Empire.*

Christian conception of family life. Paul's residence at Rome doubtless opened his eyes to the prevailing social corruption which was already threatening and undermining the stability of the imperial system. The Roman satirists have made us familiar with the painful fact that marital unfaithfulness, filial impiety, and the widespread tolerance of slavery, were the three moral cancers preying on the vitals of Roman society which was now full of festering sores. And the frescoes which are still to be seen upon many an inner wall bear witness to the unparalleled moral rottenness of that very evil age. In such a society there was urgent need to show the meaning of 'old-fashioned virtues' in the light of the Incarnation. It was far better to appear as a reactionary Jew, pleading the old religious sanctions for social purity, than to pose as an 'advanced thinker' of the type familiar to us from so much contemporary literature. None the less, why do Paul's injunctions suggest so slight a degree of reforming zeal or revolutionary change such as our modern conception of Christianity would undoubtedly demand? Why this servile attitude to such flagrant social injustices as the inferior status of womanhood, the unmerciful subjugation of childhood, and the general acceptance of slavery? Was Christianity preached only to rivet more firmly the shackles of woman, child, and slave?

The answer lies this way: First, we must readily acknowledge that the first condition of a genuine social reform is not to agitate for revolutionary change of external symptoms through external violence, but rather in the impartation of a new ideal of life which begins by changing men from within, making even the slave to triumph morally over his immoral slavery, and the down-trodden to escape from the lordship of tyranny into the larger liberty of the spirit. The slave Epictetus, who felt himself 'dear to the immortals,' even in bitter bondage, had learned this, believing as he did that God could dwell within the human body. Modern revolution (even in Russia) may turn things upside-down, and, to a limited extent, avenge the wrongs of an outrageously suppressed and offended proletariat; but it can never of itself create the new world of absolute and equal justice, or even provide adequate compensation for all the cruelty and bloodshed which are involved. Secondly, we read history to no good purpose unless we recognize that, however unobserved at the beginning, there has been descending upon human society, as the direct result of belief in the Incarnation of Christ a new power of healing and of hope which, together with its emphasis upon the value of 'things unseen,' has wrought redemption for the 'things which are seen.' External conditions, which may be reduced to ruinous heaps by revolutionary endeavours to provide new but yet unstable ground for the erection of new and more unstable edifices, may be transfigured and transformed by the light that is kindled within. The logic of the Incarnation is that men who become transformed through the indwelling presence of Christ must inevitably transfigure the institutions they control and the society of which they form a part. For illustration, consider Paul's dealing with slavery in the person of Onesimus, as reflected here and in his letter to Philemon. The institution of slavery had produced such a stratification of society that in Rome one-third of the total population was the property of the rest. Tens of thousands of men were merely live chattels, subjected daily to unspeakable barbarities, and liable at any moment by the whim of master or mistress to suffer a cruel death. Out of this iniquitous system there were but two paths, one of which ended finally in a cul-de-sac, or something worse. The other was, what appeared to so many as the one last hope; to upraise the banner of revolt, and quench in fierce blood-baths the tyranny of master over slave. And this was at any moment a terrible possibility in that old world-order; yet even the Humanists of that time were slow to reflect and pause before the menace of civil war which might utterly wreck the fabric of civilization without being able to provide even a *tabula rasa* for new experiment. History warns us that along that road lay no way even to the lower type of freedom.

But there is another course, to impatient eyes so slow, whereby Divine Love works in the hearts of men. That sense of human brotherhood in the Fatherhood of God which sprang from the Creed of the Incarnation made the slave 'the freeman of Christ' and the master 'the Lord's bondman,' yet living each for other and both for Him. It gave to all men, without distinction of condition, a common place at the altar rail; it gave the glory of a common martyrdom; it gave to the slave equally with the freeman a place in the Church's ministry. In this way came gradually but surely those very ameliorations which the 'hurry up' methods of angry men, smarting with an aggrieved sense of injustice, so frequently fail to achieve with the immediacy they crave. Who will prove that the slow ferment of a doctrine which makes men kin to the highest and partner to the best, which is the Christian method of destroying evil at its source while creating a very special quality of character, has not been vastly superior to the method of repression, whether by legalism or bloody violence, of the external symptom? To the doctrinaire of Political Science how silly, how futile, how elementary are these Pauline 'instructions'! Wives are to submit themselves to their husbands; husbands are to love their wives and not to play the 'Mr. Barrett of Wimpole Street'; children are to pay implicit obedience to their parents, and, since *fractus animus pestis juventutis*, parents are to restrain the dictatorship which causes children to lose heart; slaves are to work with a will as in the sight of God; masters are to give the square deal to their servants, remembering that they also have a Master in heaven. In short, there are two Christian principles to be observed by all: one, the obligation of duty; the other, the obligation of love. In the Christian life 'all's Law and all's Love.' One can justly claim that Christ has triumphed in many a life which has nobly accepted the painful duty of renouncing the things of this world with its many snares; nor is it too much to claim that He has triumphed still more wonderfully in the lives of humble Christian men and women who, at the cost of untold self-sacrifice, have filled the atmosphere of narrow domesticities with the light of heaven.

To know the practicability of such divine contact with the common stuff of life is to have at hand the cure for those three great problems of modern society, problems before which not only the Church but also the Law Courts seem sometimes to recoil in despair; the problem of divorce and sex relations; the problem of filial disobedience and parental indifference; and the problem of industrial injustice, restrictive practice, sabotage and slacking. Although it is not easy for the worldly-minded to believe the Church's claim that the one adequate remedy for all these problems is provided in the practical application of the doctrine of the Incarnation, yet it remains true that Christ alone has the power to lift them all into the higher atmosphere of that larger sanity which is the secret of Him, the Head over all things, and the Fullness of Him that filleth all in all.

SECTION 7.   POSITIVE INJUNCTIONS. 3 $^{1-17}$

Authorized version

1 If ye then be risen with Christ, seek those things which are above, where Christ sitteth on the right hand of God.

2 Set your affection on things above, not on things on the earth.

3 For ye are dead, and your life is hid with Christ in God.

4 When Christ, *who is* our life, shall appear, then shall ye also appear with him in glory.

5 Mortify therefore your members which are upon the earth; fornication, uncleanness, inordinate affection, evil concupiscence, and covetousness, which is idolatry:

6 For which things' sake the wrath of God cometh on the children of disobedience:

7 In the which ye also walked some time, when ye lived in them.

8 But now ye also put off all these; anger, wrath, malice, blasphemy, filthy communication out of your mouth.

9 Lie not one to another, seeing that ye have put off the old man with his deeds;

10 And have put on the new *man*, which is renewed in knowledge after the image of him that created him:

11 Where there is neither Greek nor Jew, circumcision nor uncircumcision, Barbarian, Scythian, bond *nor* free; but Christ *is* all, and in all.

12 Put on therefore, as the elect of God, holy and beloved, bowels of mercies, kindness, humbleness of mind, meekness, longsuffering;

Translation

1 Having then been raised with Christ, seek the things that are above where Christ is enthroned at God's right hand.

2 Set your hearts on things above, not on things upon the earth:

3 for you are dead: but your life is hid with Christ in God.

4 When Christ shall appear again, with whom our life is hid, then you also will appear with Him in glory.

5 Put to death, therefore, your members which are upon the earth: fornication, impurity, sensual appetite, lust, evil desire, and covetousness, which is idolatry:

6 On account of which vices the wrath of God cometh on the children of disobedience:

7 In which lusts and vices you also walked formerly, when you lived in the midst of them:

8 But now you must, in addition, put away all these—anger, wrath, malice, evil speaking, obscene talk from your mouth.

9 Lie not one to another, having put off the old man with his evil ways,

10 and having put on the new man who is renewed (re-made) by knowledge, after the image of God who created him.

11 In this 'new creation' there is neither Greek nor Jew, circumcision not uncircumcision, barbarian, Scythian, bond nor free. But Christ is all, and in all.

12 Put on therefore as the elect of God, holy and beloved, inmost compassion, kindness, humbleness of mind, meekness, long-suffering.

13 Forbearing one another, and forgiving one another, if any man have a quarrel against any: even as Christ forgave you, so also *do* ye.

14 And above all these things *put on* charity, which is the bond of perfectness.

15 And let the peace of God rule in your hearts, to the which also ye are called in one body; and be ye thankful.

16 Let the word of Christ dwell in you richly in all wisdom; teaching and admonishing one another in psalms and hymns and spiritual songs, singing with grace in your hearts to the Lord.

17 And whatsoever ye do in word or deed, *do* all in the name of the Lord Jesus, giving thanks to God and the Father by him.

13 Support one another, and forgive each other, if any has a just cause of complaint against any. Even as Christ forgave you, so also do ye.

14 Above all these things, put on love which is the bond of perfection:

15 and let the peace of Christ rule in your hearts, to which also you are called in one Body; and be thankful.

16 Let Christ's word dwell in you richly, and with all wisdom teach and admonish each other by psalms and hymns and spiritual songs, singing with grace in your hearts to the Lord.

17 And whatsoever you do in word or deed, do all in the Name of the Lord Jesus, giving thanks to God the Father through Him.

Exposition

Like many another city of the old world (and the new), Colosse had become gravely corrupt. Could anything save it from that judgement which gross immorality never fails to inflict upon a godless people? It is only as men and women learn the way of salvation through Christ that they can rise with Him to a new life. To be 'raised with Christ' is to share His lifegiving power who shares the life of God. This requires the practice of virtue and genuine piety which cannot be gained by the pursuit of earth-born and earth-bound philosophies however ingenuous. But the practice must be a perennial struggle for those who would bend their efforts Christward: it is altogether different with those who seek their values and satisfactions in the pressing solicitations of this passing world. 'Things above' are not abstract, transcendental conceptions: they are what and where Christ is enthroned in the completeness of His finished work. And they are wholly different from 'things upon the earth,' those empty honours and riches and pleasures of a perishing order. Christians are dead to this fleeting world: the crucifixion must have its counterpart in every Christian soul, and the resurrection must have its full purpose as it raises men from the moral death of sin to a life which is wholly 'hidden with Christ in God,' under His divine control, not in any transcendental other-worldliness, but in the daily moral duties which belong to the very substance of the Christian life. Living in this hard old world, the Christian never-the-less lives on the Christ-level in the midst of all workaday life. Christ is the fount of life which daily sustains the sincere Christian soul. And here is the true Mysticism—union with God which is the very life of those who are 'in Christ'; the abundant life which is life indeed, the life of love which is holiness, the Godlike life which is salvation to the uttermost.

It is worth remarking that many people have a 'hidden life' of real badness which is inwardly worse than they ever allow other people to know of, and who baffle every effort of moral reform. But Christians also have a 'hidden life' which the worldly-minded can never understand, a life from which emerges all that is fine, noble, true; all the patience, love, joy, strength, gentleness, beauty, integrity and peace of character. The springs are hidden, but replenished from a hidden source, replenished by Christ's creative cosmic energy. Thus the coming manifestation of Christ will bring with it the manifestation of all life hid with Him in God, when the outward life and the inward will be in perfect correspondence. The faith, the love, the hopes and aspirations, the ideals and noble dreams which were so often thwarted in their struggle for expression will be able to reveal themselves completely. All the 'hidden things' will come to light: the equity for which the lawyer strove will be realized; the health which the doctor sought to restore will be perfected, no longer subject to death; the ideals for which the priest has laboured will be made not merely possible but permanent; the common things of daily life will find their lasting effects: the love of parents, the sacrifice of nurses, the painstaking researches of scientists. Nothing that is true will be lost. All that ministered to God's purpose will be revealed, from the hard-won resolutions of the repentant sinner to the adoring raptures of the saint. Thus, at last, the spiritual life of the Christian soul will have its perfect glory in the medium that gives it perfect expression, in 'a body perfect and heavenly as itself' (cf. 1 Cor. 15 $^{35-49}$; 2 Cor. 5 $^{1-5}$).

Paul, however, will not allow the convert to imagine that becoming a Christian is an easy automatic guarantee of eternal salvation. Other religions may offer the easy way; but, for the Christian, life is a life-long warfare against the powers of evil. In a world confused by chaotic sensuousness the Christian alone sees those visions of the higher life which are not vouchsafed to the prosaic seekers after hedonistic satisfactions. The Christian life is a moral venture, a yearning after such perfection of character as shall prove to those 'lesser breeds without the law' that in spite of multitudinous futilities there is such fine stuff intermingled with the dross of this evil world that the Christian mind can and does transmute all baser stuff into a crown of life that never tarnishes or fades. Sexual vice, impurity, homosexual lust, *libidines praeposterae*, grasping greed, selfishness grown to a dominating passion and the worship of material things, are not limited to the old world, but they do belong to 'the old man' that lives on in every heart that is not cleansed. Even Christians are sorely tempted and assailed by that trinity of evil—the world, the flesh, and the devil. The Christian, however, is ideally a 'new man' with a 'new nature,' God's 'new creation' *in potentia*. But he must ever strive to become *de facto* what he already is ideally.

There is a stern realism in Paul's theology which never mistakes God's love for maudlin sentimentality. 'The wrath of God cometh on the children of disobedience,' not in bad-tempered retaliatory vindictiveness but in vindication of itself in the totality of its divine reaction to man's rebellion against the moral order which is inherent in the constitution of things divinely created. Sin is disruption. Man chooses it. Therefore its effect must necessarily come back upon man himself in his own character which is itself disrupted. God's wrath is the outflowing of God's holiness in a divine endeavour to restore moral principle at that point where it was broken by human rebellion: all for man's good if he will have it so, but for his undoing if he will not. Wrath and mercy are complementary factors of the Divine Love, distinguishable but not separate, contrasts but not contraries. God is one. There is no fear of 'war' in His Being.

In addition to these gross wrongs there are such common sins as anger, wrath, malice, evil talk, and obscene language. And there is the very common fault of lying, which is not only unbecoming for a Christian, but also is a sin against God as Absolute Truth.

All the evils thus condemned by Paul still characterize the lower nature of man, and although the catalogue might well be enlarged in this mid-twentieth century, they are just the things that separate man from God and that work the worst evils of man upon his fellows. But Paul also shows that moral evil has no further terrors when Christ dwells within. Once the 'new birth' has taken place, a 'new character' is already in the course of formation, and man's re-creation in Christ makes him what God first designed him to be. The re-making is indeed a renewal. Furthermore, in Christ and this 'new creation' old unhappy distinctions become non-existent. Racial, religious, and social differences are all man-made, and therefore they also need to be redeemed. Christ is Saviour of each and all; our common centre, our gravitational pull which holds our common life together from disintegration. The Christ-nature is communicated to all men in all places of the world, so that no man, whatever his country, condition, or colour, is excluded from the benefit and blessedness of the re-newed nature, if he will but accept Christ's redemption. There may be *apartheid* in Africa, but there is none in Christ. Little Rock of the United States of America may fight over it, but not upon *that* rock has Jesus built His Church against which 'the gates of hell shall not prevail.' All must pay homage to His universal Lordship, and submit to the reconciling unity of His kingdom. In establishing truth and combating error the Cross of Christ is the bond by which all union is cemented, and the force by which all opposing powers are vanquished. Christians are to live as God's 'chosen ones' who are to show themselves as such by the quality of their life. Holiness, a heart of compassion, the kindness which is a delicate consideration for others, humbleness of mind which is lowliness and never loftiness, meekness which is gentleness and never self-assertion, longsuffering which does not complain, forbearance which is devoid of anger or irritation, forgiveness which ever shows forth grace in suffering injustice rather than in inflicting it, and above all love which is the substance of all Christian virtues as it is also the bond of perfection and the crown of all Christian endeavour; these are the qualities which every Christian must seek to achieve if the 'peace of Christ' is to rule in men's hearts as the source of all inner tranquillity and loveliness of soul, and as the final security against every threat of evil. Christians can rely utterly upon 'the word of Christ' to inspire, direct, control, enrich, for here is the true Wisdom for those who are beset by intellectual problems as well as by moral choices. Here is something to sing about, for Christianity is the religion of Redemption and Joy. Christianity covers all the practical activities of daily life, and in Christ's will can everything be done as a thankoffering to God the Father.

SECTION 8. FAMILY DUTIES. 3 ¹⁸–4 ¹

Authorized Version

18 Wives, submit yourselves unto your own husbands, as it is fit in the Lord.

19 Husbands, love *your* wives, and be not bitter against them.

20 Children, obey *your* parents in all things: for this is well pleasing unto the Lord.

21 Fathers, provoke not your children *to anger*, lest they be discouraged.

22 Servants, obey in all things *your* masters according to the flesh; not with eyeservice, as menpleasers; but in singleness of heart, fearing God:

23 And whatsoever ye do, do *it* heartily, as to the Lord, and not unto men;

24 Knowing that of the Lord ye shall receive the reward of the inheritance: for ye serve the Lord Christ.

25 But he that doeth wrong shall receive for the wrong which he hath done: and there is no respect of persons.

iv. 1 Masters, give unto *your* servants that which is just and equal; knowing that ye also have a Master in heaven.

Translation

18 Wives, be subject to your own husbands, as is fit in the Lord.

19 Husbands, love your wives, and be not bitter against them.

20 Children, obey your parents in everything, for this is well-pleasing in the Lord.

21 Fathers, do not exasperate your children, lest they become dispirited.

22 Servants, obey in all things your masters according to the flesh, not with eye-service, as men-pleasers, but with integrity of heart, as fearing the Lord;

23 and whatever you do, do it with all your will, as working to the Lord and not to men only:

24 knowing that from the Lord you shall receive the just recompense of the inheritance, for you are serving the Lord Christ.

25 For he who does unjustly will receive for the injustice he has done; and there is no respect of persons.

iv. 1. Masters, show your servants what is just and equal, knowing that you also have a Master in the Heavens.

Exposition

Following upon his great thesis of the Cosmic Christ, Paul realizes that everything cosmic needs to be redeemed. Society needs redemption, and, since the family is the unit of society, only the Christianized family can make society what Christ wishes it to be.

It is interesting to observe that in each of the three family relations which Paul deals with, the subordinate party is the first addressed, and the duty of Christian submission is primarily insisted upon. There may have been a particular reason for this in the state of the Asiatic Churches or of Greek society in that region; but other indications suggest that Paul sought to check the dangers of un-settlement in the natural relations of family and social life following upon the inevitable change towards spiritual liberty. Observe how 'the Lord' and His authority are to be regarded as the higher sanction for each of these natural duties. The wife-husband relationship must be properly grounded, despite all feminist movements towards so-called emancipation; and although authority belongs to the husband, the rule of love is always better than the love of rule. Rigour is out of place in the Christian home, and love must be ἀγαπάω, a word which expresses the highest spiritual value of true devotion. Experience proves that it is not always so, and there is often an *odium amori mixtum*, a surly discontent which causes much domestic exasperation and alienates all affection. Again, Paul's word to children, 'obey your parents in everything,' a word which seems so out-dated, needs to be restored to our modern family life. A revival of this elementary Christian principle is urgently required in an age when rebellious teen-agers, Teddy-boys and Teddy-girls alike, threaten to disrupt and undermine the foundations of whole-some family life. 'Honour thy father and thy mother' is a principle which it would be very profitable to recover. The law of filial obedience has its creative ground 'in the Lord' and is an essential part of the Christian order of life, which is but the *natural* order restored and perfected. On the other hand there is Paul's necessary injunction to fathers: 'don't exasperate your children' by nagging complaints and criticisms which so easily produces a sickening discouragement in the docile child and a slumbering resentment in the sensitive. The world can never know how many young hearts have been broken by an irritable parent, or how many fathers have turned themselves into enemies by their unreasoning exactions.

The Christian principle applies to every relationship. Servants should obey their masters, not as clock-watchers, nor as men-pleasers, nor as doing only that which is calculated to catch the eye of the master—which leads to duplicity when the master's eye is not looking that way. Integrity in service is essential: he who would serve truly must put his 'very soul' into all his work as the fullest expression of his Christian personality. The workman who loves Christ will find both the humblest and the hardest task dignified by offering it as part of his daily dedication to his Lord. It is work that is devoid of the Christian ideal of service that tends towards the lower standards of work deprived of honesty and thoroughness. The idea of 'bondage' must become the ideal of moral responsibility. The Christian knows nothing of 'restrictive practices.' And the true workman, though entitled to a just recompense for his services, is much more concerned with that Christian inheritance which is his legacy won by Christ. For a slave to be heir of anything was the most ennobling paradox of early Christian thought, and the secret of the paradox lies here—'for you serve the Lord Christ.'

The problem of justice is not new: it is as old as human relationships. Paul gives a universal warning: 'he who does unjustly will receive for the injustice he has done; there is no respect of persons.' There is no excuse for wrongdoing by 'the boss.' Nor will his domineering spirit afford any excuse to the idle, go-slow, work-to-rule, unfaithful servant. Tyranny is nowadays a two-edged sword that cleaves asunder many good relations between the owners of the business in the Board-Room and the shop-stewards on the floor. But there are no favouritisms with Christ. 'No-one is accepted at his face-value' (οὐκ ἔστιν προσωπολημψία). The tyrant, whatever his class, station, or condition, will 'receive again the wrong he did.' Like a boomerang, evil returns to him who sets it in motion. Mutual respect and just and equitable reward are required of servants and masters alike. Justice without equity is the precursor of much dispute and disruption. Jesus Himself laid down the principle of equity bearing on all human relations (*Luke* 6 [31]). It was germinal of the abolition of slavery then, as it must be of colour-bar and similar iniquities now. Moral equity when fully realized by Christian conscience must inevitably lead on to complete equality before the law. The Cosmic Christ is Master of masters and Lord of lords, in whom our Sociology will yet find the solution that is the perfected social part of man's total salvation.

Such ideas had never been heard before, ideas which would have been scouted by the highest and most ethical philosophy. The idea of one common humanity in Christ, which was quite a new conception, underlies the whole. There is but one true Body of which all are members. If that ideal could be realized, men

I

could not wrong one another without gravely wronging themselves. Certainly most of the evils of the past could have been avoided had this Christian conception of life been more earnestly accepted. Its practice now would solve our greatest problems and meet most of the evils of our time. Yet men are slow to learn the way of true life which is life lived to God and going forth to man in the spirit of Christ who is the Way, the Truth, and the Life that God *is*. A new ethical life can only come from a new spiritual life which is the essential thing in Christianity.

The Christian life has always been essentially the same in kind and quality, and it is still the 'new life' as compared and contrasted with the ordinary life of the world. We are not born into it by nature; we must be born again of a higher purpose and by voluntary choice if we are to pass from the power of the passing world. It is a life of devotion to God and to all that He is. Life is the one great possibility given to all men. Apart from purely theological questions, the great concern of every man born into this world is what his life shall be. The supreme value of the Christian religion is that in Christ the possibility of rising to a life that is divine and eternal is set before us. For this, God has created us, and to this He has redeemed us. Only by obeying the call in Christ can we be lifted above ourselves to that which is the true life of God in man; and only as this life is lived in the world and for the world's highest good, as Christ Himself lived it, can the world be blest. Yet it is not merely a choice that is asked of us, as if by an act of our own will we could raise ourselves into this higher life. It is a *response to God* as He comes reconciling us to Himself in Christ, a reception of the Divine Spirit as He comes to us through Christ and as the spiritual power of God is centred in Him for our life. It is through this response to God in Christ, this reception of Christ as that which He is to us, and for us, and in us, that the new spiritual power is vouchsafed which is the inspiration and strength of the new life, the abundant life that is life indeed. While, apart from a personal relation to Christ, Christianity approves itself ethically as the right life-choice, only that Christianity in which Christ is central will prove effective in experience, and only by faith in Him do we stand in the Christian succession.

CHAPTER IV

CONCLUDING EXHORTATIONS AND GREETINGS

Analysis

Section 9. 4 $^{2-6}$

Brief exhortations concerning prayer and social conduct.

Section 10. 4 $^{7=17}$

Personal messages and Greetings.

Section 11. 4 ^{18}

Paul now seals his Epistle with his own authenticating signature and final benediction.

Introduction

In order to make his practical admonitions the more complete, Paul recommends perseverance in prayer, with due thanksgiving, as the best means of obtaining divine help for all the actual difficult tasks of daily life (verse 2).

Praying thus for themselves, Paul bids them to pray for him and his fellow-labourers, that God would grant them new opportunities to preach 'the mystery of Christ,' for which he was now 'in bonds' (verse 3); and courage to preach it in that uncompromising manner which became him whom Christ had made His apostle to the Gentiles (verse 4).

Continuing, he counsels the Colossians to avoid provoking the pagans by any imprudent display of their new-found zeal, but so to conduct themselves as to avoid persecution, and so gain time to spread the Gospel (verse 5). And in particular, when conversing with unbelievers, to make their discourse gentle and courteous, but at the same time to make it wholesome with wisdom and truth, that they might be able to give the right answer to any who inquired about their faith (verse 6).

From these general instructions it is natural to pass to the personal references which, in the light of what has been already said, will in no way be looked upon as mere addenda. The great and all-important question as to whether Christ is truly reigning in the world of men is answered affirmatively, not through high-sounding systems of so-called philosophy, but by just such tests as these personal references afford. Take, for example, the first two, namely, the greetings concerning Tychicus and Onesimus (verses 7, 8, 9). In some imperfect manifestations of Christianity the underlings of the saints—slaves, servants, bondmen—have fared but ill. Yet here is Tychicus, a subordinate, a mere letter-carrier, who nevertheless is glorified with the humble service he performs for the furtherance of the Gospel. He has learned by heart, so to speak, the clause which 'makes drudgery divine.' His whole career, though missing earthly fame during his lifetime, is immortalized because of the apparently trivial service done in Christ's name. As a consequence we see him linked with Paul himself as 'a beloved brother,' 'a faithful minister,' 'a fellow bondman.' Many a millionaire, many a man distinguished and rewarded by grateful potentates and adorned with titles, might well envy Tychicus his secure place in human history. A still more striking case is that of Onesimus. A frightened runaway slave, guilty no doubt of idleness, lying, thievery, deceit, a profitless chattel, he has been rescued, through the practical application of a certain *new theory of human nature*, from the lowest degradation that human nature was capable of enduring. Lifted out of the mire by this new 'social science' of the doctrine of Incarnate Love, Onesimus too has risen to fellowship with Paul, and is now become 'a faithful and beloved brother.' Similar significance beautifies the remaining salutations. First, we are brought into touch with three large-hearted Christian Jews, Aristarchus, Marcus (now purged of his early failure), and Jesus Justus (verses 10, 11). These have been a comfort to Paul in his imprisonment. Then there is Epaphras the evangelist of Colosse, with a splendid tribute to his labour on behalf of his home town (verses 12, 13). Then come those two distinguished Gentile associates, Dr. Luke 'the beloved physician,' and Demas (verse 14) who, alas, was to become even more distinguished by his subsequent defection: 'Demas hath forsaken me, having loved this present world.'

The final messages are in no way out of harmony with the thought which has been emphasized. The brethren in Laodicea are cordially remembered: also Nympha and the brethren who gathered at her house (verse 15).

Then follows a 'directive,' as we should call it to-day, which throws considerable light on the way in which the Pauline Epistles obtained circulation: that when the Epistle to the Colossians had been read, it (or perhaps a copy) is to be forwarded to the Church at Laodicea. At the same time the Epistle sent to the Laodiceans is to be sent on to Colosse (verse 16). Allusion has already been made to the question as to whether this last-named Epistle represents one known to us under another name, e.g., the Epistle to the Ephesians; or whether, through that lukewarmness with which the Laodiceans are charged in the Apocalypse, it was allowed to perish.

The last personal greeting is to Archippus (verse 17) who was probably the ordained son of Philemon, urging him to give 'full heed' to his ministry. Are we to suppose, from the tender seriousness of Paul's message, that this young man's zeal has been declining? It is hardly necessary to make such a supposition, as many scholars have done, seeing here a sharp rebuke. The simple fact appears to be that the grand old missionary (as in his letter to Timothy) is gravely anxious that they to whom such 'fullness' has been committed as a stewardship should not themselves fail in 'fullness' of witness. 'Take heed to the ministry which thou hast received in the Lord, that thou fulfil it.' What young man, pondering upon the significance of his divine calling and Ordination, could fail to be solemnized at the responsibility before God and man which the sacred ministry received from the reigning Christ imposed upon him? Must not every labourer for Christ consecrate himself over and over again with renewed ardour to fulfil the ministry which has been thus received?

The Epistle is completed. So Paul now takes the reed from the hand of his amanuensis to add, according to his custom, the final salutation. As the chains clank together in falling upon the desk before him, he inscribes in his customary 'large letters' the last pathetic appeal, gathering up the whole witness of his career in the word: 'Remember my bonds,' and the whole purport of his message in the prayer: 'Grace be with you. Amen' (verse 18). *Grace*—the meaning of that Divine Love which reached down into chaos from highest heaven to indwell the lowest abyss. The *Pleroma*, the Fullness of Perfection, is not unreachable by man, and the material world is not irredeemable. Man in Christ is the potential master of both his worlds, undefiled by matter, undismayed by the, as yet, 'far off divine event to which the whole creation moves'; far off maybe, yet surely mounting to the ever-beckoning height wherein God dwells. Life is from henceforth informed and energized by the wondrous miracle that, as the completion of the existence of the Infinite is to be found in its contact with the Finite, so likewise the destiny of Man is alone to be discerned in that Infinite to which the Christ lifts up his being.

SECTION 9. BRIEF EXHORTATIONS CONCERNING PRAYER AND SOCIAL CONDUCT. 4 $^{2-6}$

Authorized Version

2 Continue in prayer, and watch in the same with thanksgiving;

3 Withal praying also for us, that God would open unto us a door of utterance, to speak the mystery of Christ, for which I am also in bonds:

4 That I may make it manifest, as I ought to speak.

5 Walk in wisdom toward them that are without, redeeming the time.

6 Let your speech *be* alway with grace, seasoned with salt, that ye may know how ye ought to answer every man.

Translation

2 Continue steadfast in prayer, watching thereunto with thanksgiving.

3 At the same time pray for us also, that God would open to us a door for the word, to speak the Mystery of Christ, for which I am even in bonds;

4 that I may make it manifest, as it becomes me to speak.

5 Walk in wisdom towards them who are without, redeeming the time.

6 Let your speech be always with grace, seasoned with salt, knowing how you ought to answer everybody.

Exposition

Prayer and watchful continuance and steadfast zeal are essential to a full Christian life. There is plenty to be thankful for. Intercession also for others is an essential part of Christian life and duty, not that the stewards may be relieved of hardship but that the Lord would open new doors of opportunity for work and witness. Clergy and people to-day could learn a useful lesson here—clergy should not be too self-sufficient to ask the assistance of their people's prayers: laity should gladly provide this spiritual support through their faithful intercessions. The mystery of Christ needs still to be revealed in the modern situation, disclosed, unfolded, made an open secret, the unsearchable riches freely distributed. Similarly,

Christians are to behave Christianly towards 'them who are without,' lest zeal and piety become an occasion of offence. The superior attitude is as unwise as it is undesirable. 'With prudence grasp every opportunity for Christ which the occasion affords you: make the most of it: we live in a momentous time.' It is possible to be wilful and so ruin your influence: but it is also possible to be winningly impressive. It is not necessary for the Christian to emulate those whose speech is pungent, witty, caustic, like the Greeks of the early days who were adepts at this kind of conversation and which won the title 'Attic salt!' Christian also have a salt—speech that is flavoured with Christ's grace. It is this that keeps wisdom pure and conversation uncorrupt.

It should never be forgotten that the gift of speech to man was the direct outcome of the infusion of God's spirit. Hence the warning: 'By thy words shalt thou be justified, and by thy words shalt thou be condemned.' This also needs to be restored to a world in which loose talk and bad language are definitely increasing, and adding to the world's evil.

SECTION 10. CONCLUDING MESSAGES AND GREETINGS. 4 $^{7-17}$

Authorized Version

7 All my state shall Tychicus declare unto you, *who is* a beloved brother, and a faithful minister and fellow-servant in the Lord:

8 Whom I have sent unto you for the same purpose, that he might know your estate, and comfort your hearts:

9 With Onesimus, a faithful and beloved brother, who is *one* of you. They shall make known unto you all things which *are done* here.

10 Aristarchus my fellowprisoner saluteth you, and Marcus, sister's son to Barnabas, (touching whom ye received commandments: if he come unto you, receive him;)

11 And Jesus, which is called Justus, who are of the circumcision. These only *are my* fellowworkers unto the kingdom of God, which have been a comfort unto me.

Translation

7 Everything concerning me will be made known to you by Tychicus, a beloved brother, a faithful minister and fellow-servant in the Lord:

8 whom I have sent to you for this very purpose, so that you may know our affairs, and that he may comfort your hearts:

9 together with Onesimus, a loyal and beloved brother, who is from you. They will tell you all that is done here.

10 Aristarchus my fellow-prisoner sends you Greetings, and Marcus (Barnabas's sister's son) about whom you received orders. If he comes to you, make him welcome:

11 and so does Jesus who is called Justus. They are of the Circumcision. These also are labourers with me in the Kingdom of God, who have been a consolation to me.

12 Epaphras, who is *one* of you, a servant of Christ, saluteth you, always labouring fervently for you in prayers, that ye may stand perfect and complete in all the will of God.

13 For I bear him record, that he hath a great zeal for you, and them *that are* in Laodicea, and them in Hierapolis.

14 Luke, the beloved physician, and Demas, greet you.

15 Salute the brethren which are in Laodicea, and Nymphas, and the church which is in his house.

16 And when this epistle is read among you, cause that it be read also in the church of the Laodiceans; and that ye likewise read the *epistle* from Laodicea.

17 And say to Archippus, Take heed to the ministry which thou hast received in the Lord, that thou fulfil it.

12 Epaphras, who is one of yourselves, a true slave of Christ, greets you at all times fervently striving for you by prayers that you may stand fast, perfect and completed in the whole will of God.

13 For I bear him witness that he has worked hard for you, and for them in Laodicea as also in Hierapolis.

14 Dear Doctor Luke and Demas send you Greetings.

15 Salute the brethren in Laodicea, and Nymphas and the church in his (or more probably 'her') house.

16 And when this Epistle has been read to you, cause that it be read also in the church of the Laodiceans: and that you also read the one from Laodicea:

17 and say to Archippus: Take heed to the ministry which you have received in the Lord, that you may fulfil it.

Exposition

Although Paul's concluding messages and greetings are personal, they are not unimportant as having a wider aspect. For behind brief references lay a rare example to all Christian people, especially those committed to the work of the holy ministry. Tychicus an Asian is now with Paul in prison, but about to be sent home to tell the home church of missionary advance, of Paul's constancy in preaching the Gospel, his sufferings, the bitter opposition, the progress made, the imprisonment and the literary efforts. This kind of thing is still the inspiration of the Church, and will ever be required so long as missionary endeavour continues. It is as up to date as the latest Report of our various Missionary societies, and is as great a challenge to the home base as it ever was. The story is still one of imprisoned dignitaries, of runaway slaves like Onesimus lifted from the deeper slavery of sin to the Christian level of life, of persecuted Jews like Aristarchus and Caius, of Cypriots like Barnabas, faithful to the glorious cause like Epaphras and 'dear Dr. Luke.' And, alas, there is many a Demas too who fails and sinks back into 'this present world.' But there is also many a Nympha, women of social standing whose hospitable homes are indeed a comfort to the Church as to its tired workers in the field. Not least there is the curate-in-charge, Archippus, the lonely young man, to be remembered and encouraged to fulfil his ministry in a completely consecrated self-offering.

SECTION II. PAUL SEALS THE EPISTLE WITH HIS OWN AUTHENTI-
CATING SIGNATURE AND FINAL BENEDICTION. 4 [18]

Authorized Version	*Translation*
18 The salutation by the hand of me Paul. Remember my bonds. Grace *be* with you. Amen.	18 My own Greetings I write with my own hand and my own signature. Remember my bonds. Grace be with you all.—PAUL.

Exposition

Paul is now an old man. His eyesight is failing, so 'with large letters' he writes his salutation: 'Remember my bonds'—four years' imprisonment for the Gospel's sake, innumerable hardships, desperate dangers, chains. Nothing more is wanting in order to confirm the world in the belief that Christ is Lord indeed, Lord of all Creation, the very Christ of God and the redeeming Christ of Man, the Christ-Redeemer of the whole mysterious Cosmic Order.

PART II

FINAL QUESTION: AND ANSWER

They dig in the earth for the heavy atoms,
And delve for the laws of the nucleus.
With cunning devices they measure its rays:
The isotopes they separate with uncanny skill—
Unwearying the labours, infinite the pains,
When they seek the secrets of Matter.
Toying with Death at their finger-tips,
They tinker with the hidden power of the Cosmos—
While the Devil rubs his technical hands.

Yet how to separate the Evil from the Good
Their quantum theory knows not.
To search the precious secrets of the Spirit,
This research has never wearied them.
Thy holy laws they never seek,
On the Celestial Radiance never gaze.
Nor can they find that mightier Power
Who frowns on their presumption,
And who, because He loves the meek,
Will take the wise
In their own craftiness.

DAVID WATSON

(*Life and Work:* The Record of the Church of Scotland.   October 1959, p. 184)

FINAL QUESTION: AND ANSWER

LORD BERTRAND RUSSELL has somewhere stated his belief that 'our modern world is dying of cosmic impiety.' If this judgement is correct, the question arises: Is there anyone or anything that can save us from a situation which could so easily lead to cosmic disaster? The Christian Church finds the answer in the *Cosmic Christ*, and that He alone is adequate to meet our desperate need. That is the Christian claim. But the further question at once emerges: Is this faith really, truly, and wholly adequate for our day? For example, in view of modern scientific concepts concerning the astro-physical universe,[1] can we rightly speak of the Cosmic Christ at all, or of Christ as Lord of the expanding universe of galaxies and incredible distances measured in multi-millions of light-years: of Christ as the Creator and Upholder of the whole vast Order 'visible and invisible, of things created, of things in the making and of things that are being continuously created'? Again, is the Pauline doctrine of the *Pleroma* equal to the problems that confront our time, or must we, in sheer intellectual honesty, discard it as a religious theory that, whatever it originally meant, has completely lost its relevance? Or does it, peradventure, offer an insight that we urgently need, as a thread of light to guide us through the bewildering confusions of to-day?

Twice in a period of twenty-five years has our generation, exhausted and mutilated by war, witnessed the collapse of every prop upon which our civilization had hitherto depended: financial solidarity, the community of labour, reason, alliances, armaments, banking, modernism, gold-standard, traditionalism, monetary reform, pacts, combines, sanctions, diplomacy, propaganda, and the balance of power. Whilst all our political chatterers and sentimental idealogues were bending the knee to these false gods, every man held to and inculcated his own particular doctrine in the belief

---

[1] See A. C. B. Lovell's *Reith Lectures* 1958: The Individual and the Universe; and, for the non-technical reader, Dr. R. A. Lyttleton's illuminating series in *The Illustrated London News* (1959): The Universe at the beginning of the Space Age.

that his chosen 'graven image' would obligingly incline its head. Meanwhile, unlike the great composers of music and poetry, who thought deeply about people, life, love, laughter, sorrow, suffering, death, and the great Beyond, and of aesthetic theory as it impinged upon these elementals, the politicians exercised no such creativity, because they saw humanity through a glass darkly, or at least in a light that was deeply dimmed by lack of political comprehension; for when politicians fail to find any vital interest in the philosophy of their own particular science, and think of it as the computation of votes rather than the elucidation of principles, the people perish. Thus all these ideas and hopes have been trusted, all have been tried, and all have failed to bring peace to the world or goodwill to men. Theories and policies and expediencies have been swept aside by the very forces which we fondly imagined would hold the world together but which proved impotent to do so.

In addition to these, we believed there were other forces that could not fail. Did not this self-same Paul proclaim from Mars Hill that 'God has made of one blood all nations of men for to dwell upon the earth,' and has also determined the bounds of their habitation? That is indeed a truth which may well shock our aristocratic vanity: but go back twenty generations, and every man can discover for himself more than a hundred thousand ancestors; go back fifty generations, and he will find more than five million foresires. There is not in Western Europe a single neolithic relic that is not a family relic of every one of us. Truly we are akin. Yet the bonds of flesh and blood cannot hold the world together, much less bring in the kingdom of heaven. From the clash of race and colour to the contentions of the Divorce Courts: the 'haves' warring with the 'haves-not': the riot of lust, passion, envy, hatred, greed—our world looks more like a discordant struggling mass of lunatics with nothing to hold it together, than a large human family held together by reason, education, understanding, mutual charity, and forbearance.

Again, many serious and sober-minded thinkers considered that civilization itself had brought mankind to a point of moral excellence, to a degree of reciprocity, where it would never again resort to brute force to advance its interests or settle its disputes. A vain hope indeed, as modern events abundantly prove.

Others thought that the amazing victories of Science would usher in an era of universal happiness beyond all human dreams. Medicine, surgery, and biological research would combine to reduce disease and lengthen life. Indeed, man's whole outlook and happiness would be ensured by the manufacture of synthetic drugs in a painless world. But science, so far from uniting mankind, places ever new and more deadly instruments of destruction in the hands of men, making slaughter not only more terrible than ever before, but potentially encompassing the death of the world itself. Dr. Wand (former Bishop of London) writing in the *Church Times* of April 24th, 1959 (p. 15) says: 'Ever since the scientists introduced us to the theory of Relativity, we seem to have lost our moorings. As there is no fixed point in this universe, so we have thought that there is no fixed standard anywhere. The sense of the absolute by which our fathers set such store seems to have disappeared from almost every walk of life. The historian gives up his emphasis on the truth of facts: the moralist retreats from his insistence on standards: the psychologist has dissolved personality into an eddy in the stream of consciousness. No wonder the Teddy-boy and the juvenile delinquent fail to see why they should try to be good and obey the law. The shifting urge of physical desires has a more obvious claim to satisfaction.' It is, of course, a fact that our science has outstripped our morality: hence our mental and moral instability. The progress of the one has not kept pace with the progress of the other. It is, accordingly, a terrible indictment on our way of living that so many of our leading scientists are expected to expend their brilliant talents devising more deadly engines of destruction when the most vital need of mankind is the preservation of life's richest values. Consequently we are faced with the choice, so sharply are the issues now divided, between *Life* and *Death*. Unless every new discovery of Truth is made to serve the purpose of God, it will assuredly serve only to destroy man. But the world is slow to believe that the way of Peace is never found with Herod.

Again, Education, in which so many doctrinaires, pedants and eclectics trusted, also failed to hold the world together. Indeed, the nations that were locked in death-grapple on the blood-soaked fields of war were the most highly cultivated and learned of the modern world. Education may train men, but unless in the future it is to be of a different kind and with different aims, it cannot of itself bind men together. Why not? Because there is such a thing in this world as Evil which, whatever the origin of this mystery, is a real force which cannot be easily exorcized by an educational 'system' or a few equalitarian Acts of Parliament or dictatorial Orders in Council.

Similarly, Commerce cannot hold men and nations together. Times without number our statisticians assured us that the war we feared would never come because the unseen empire of Finance would not tolerate it. Brilliant theses were brilliantly argued by men of commanding intellect supported by masses of facts and figures to prove that war never pays because its advantages, even to the victors, are illusory. Two world-wars have not disproved the facts on which the arguments were based. But war itself is a fact; and we now know that nations will fight regardless of cost, because some things are reckoned priceless; and that some nations will deliberately go to war, nuclear bombs or no, to defend or to extend their commercial interests. Theories often fail in the face of stark reality.

But other influences overflowing with facile optimism contributed nothing but a record of unrelieved failure to stave off world war. Socialism, with its vague humanitarian mysticism and its glowing rhetoric of a cosmopolitan philosophy backed by golden promises of lavish dispensations of public hospitality, collapsed like a house of cards in a storm. 'Brother' went to war with 'brother,' and 'comrade' slaughtered 'comrade.' So was it with Humanism and its abstract idealisms excogitated by philosophers of ultra-liberal leanings and dreamland panaceas. Worse still, the Church failed too: having lost the vision of the Cosmic Christ, it lost its power to uplift and guide the nations, or to draw men together in His charity, basing human life on love and therefore on service plus sacrifice. Split into countless sects more schismatic than any State, the Church could not hold itself together, despite its ecumenical yearnings for unity. Christian murdered Christian.

Shall we plough again this barren soil, or be again projected into what may prove to be a still more deadly morass from which there will be no deliverance at all? Have the millions of cross-crowned graves taught us nothing? Have the fields of war brought forth only poppies?

Manifestly, then, this at least is clear: our race cannot be held together by outward pressures. It must therefore find its centre of amity in some inward spiritual nucleus of life. And here lies our clue. If we are to find the ultimate unity which underlies all creeds and overarches all sects and the diversities of humanity, we must seek it, not in the welter of secular interests but in the Divine Life which encompasses us whilst it indwells us. Far above the cruel fields of war, far below the ceaseless din of a world that is too much with us, higher than all sects, deeper than all dogmas, there is a life of the Spirit common to all mankind, potential in all, realized by few, and only as much as our bewildered human race is lifted into that life of invincible goodwill can it attain to enduring unity and peace. But, alas, there are clear signs that the unregenerate world of to-day is fast hardening down again into a system of bristling nationalities, each seeking to exalt itself on the basis of material strength and war-preparedness. Consequently we are in immediate danger of taking an international backspring to all those evil ways which two world-wars were fought to obliterate from out future life. Thus we are threatened with a system of society that finds its animation in the lust for power, the spirit of gain, the hardness that is steeled against the needs of others, and the aggressiveness that refuses to let sentiment stand in the way. Therefore so long as these qualities hold sway, so long must the world remain what sin and selfishness have made it. Under whatever system of government, or by whatever name it bears, the world can be no better, no cleaner, no saner, no safer, no sweeter, than the hearts and minds of the men and women who compose the world. It is the *new* humanity, the *redeemed* humanity, that will make a new world for a redeemed society to live in. The Cosmic Christ alone has the Cosmic Love which can embrace all human spirits; and the solidarity of mankind can be realized only as we discover our true kinship in fellowship with Him. If this seems vague at first, we have but to ponder it in the face of all the facts about us, and not least within us, to learn that, after all, it is not only good theology but also the only sound practical reality.

Mercifully there are influences in the world, of which the Cross of Christ is the changeless symbol, mightier than armies, vaster in their sweep, and more irresistible than the ruffian forces that destroy. There are 'things that cannot be shaken,' though empires fall and cultures crumble; and at last, if not by wisdom, then by tragedy, mankind will learn where lie the holy foundations upon which to build its habitation of Comradeship, its palace of Justice, and its temple of Faith. It becomes increasingly clear that if the spirit of Christ, His truth, His laws, are not to be the permanent principles of society, there is no civilization to be relied upon. The divine alone unites: evil divides. And only as men yield their hearts to His spirit can they be drawn into a union of true brotherhood, a union of those who love in the service of those who need. The Sermon on the Mount, long regarded as too idealistic and unworkable, reads, in the light of to-day's poignant need, more like the Magna Charta of civilization. But men reject it for lesser ideologies. Similarly, an age that spurns the Pauline gospel of Justification by Faith finds nowhere any justification for faith. And here lies the absolute agnosticism that darkens so many minds to-day, amongst which are to be found the most intelligent, impeccable and upright of our generation, both male and female: novelists, litterateurs, scientists, lawyers, journalists, editors, doctors, teachers, business men, professors, students. The creeds which nurtured their fathers they find no longer credible or even intelligible. The simple fact is, of course, that there is much in religion that is quite unintelligible until belief opens the eyes of the understanding. As William James put it: 'Like all things that demand risk, Christianity can only be understood from inside.' Yet these people are not irreligious. Although they make, as they say, 'no profession of belief,' they are very fruitful in performances of good works, some of which have won universal acclaim. Thus men of science, men of letters, men of high inventive genius, men of affairs, men aglow with social idealism and humanitarian effort, stand aloof from the Church, affirming that they neither need it nor are helped by it. Time was when the task of the Church was to convert bad men; now it strives to retain the good ones. Once the Church supported men in life's fierce struggle, upholding the heavy-laden and comforting the sorrow-bound: now men are besought by every means to support the Church in her anxious struggle to survive. But why? Why do the very people who have the future in their hearts stand apart? Are we to throw the historic dogmas of the Church out of the window and start all over again? Start where? What is it that will satisfy not only the intellectual integrity of the educated but also the deep yearning of our nature and the needs that gnaw our hearts? Obviously something profoundly convincing is needed if men and women are to be directed to what we Christians affirm to be the only True Light; for it is a deeply disturbing fact that men and women will turn, and do turn, in their dire perplexities to the craziest superstitions, to the crudest dogmas, accepting wonders which pure intellect rejects for the solace which intellect alone cannot provide.

What answer can the Christian Church give to this disturbing fact? It may well lie this way: when we who profess and call ourselves Christians seriously dare to believe in the religion we profess, and have the courage to lay it to heart and live it out in all the actual, practical, difficult tasks of daily life with all its testings, we shall not lack the power to convince others that we have the only truth that has personal relevance for human beings.

This, however, involves other questions: Is our faith based on a genuine personal experience, or is it an easy-going contentment based on an undisturbed and unexamined convention? Christians, above all others, must never be people of negative pliability, nor yet of an unintelligent piety only, but people possessed of those strong qualities and virtues which have so greatly lost prestige in our own times. Let every man look into his own heart and mind, clearly, honestly, unflinchingly, and he will find there the cause and the remedy for the woes of the world; for whatever promotes discord within ourselves is writ large in the strife of humanity. By the same token, if we seek that which holds our own life together we shall find the essential secret, for society is only two or more or very many more people like ourselves trying to live together in the world at the same time. What, then, do we find when we look within, seeking the deepest fact hidden in this strange entity we call the human soul? We discover there, amongst much that is distressing, perhaps even surprising and not a little alarming, a *law of love* and the immutable duty of obedience to that law as the only way to the larger sanity and the blessed life. Such pure and unblemished joy as we experience on this earth, as every honest soul can testify, comes of obedience to that sovereignty whose authority we cannot doubt and whose appeal we cannot hush. Not one of us but has learned that selfish living is a fragmentary life, fretful, futile, truncated, weary, miserable. The day of days, the great day of the feast of life, is when we yield ourselves, not to the sway

of some all-controlling human passion but to an all-redeemin
Person who reconciles and adjudicates amongst our warring motive
and shifts the centre of life from self to God. Then the pre-eminer
truth is realized in our experience: that Christ is indeed the redeem
of man, in whose spirit we find both concentration of self and escap
from self; in a word, salvation.

The need of appreciating the full significance of the doctrine
Christ is as great to-day as ever. The all-sufficiency of the mediatori
work of Christ is still the solution to our human problems and th
answer to every doubt, for, as in the time of Paul, we are constantl
confronted by inadequate presentations of the Christian Faith suc
as obscure the essential message of Christ to the world, with th
result that many of to-day's vagaries, new as they sometimes seen
are only revivals of the vagaries of yesterday, and the materiali
Occident repeats again and again the speculations of the theosophi
Orient. For all these, as pertinently now as over nineteen centurie
ago, the answer is in the proclamation of that truth to which Pai
bears witness and to which we pay instinctive reverence as w
repeat the affirmation of the Nicene Creed:

> One Lord, Jesus Christ, the only-begotten Son of God,
> Begotten of His Father before all worlds,
> God of God, Light of Light, Very God of Very God,
> Begotten, not made: Being of one substance with the Father,
> By whom all things were made;
> Who for us men and for our salvation came down from heaven,
> And was incarnate by the Holy Ghost, of the Virgin Mary,
> And was made man.

Now that, of course, is pure dogma. But no dogma was eve
invented: every doctrine of the Church was originally an effor
to utter and interpret a deep and vital reality of experience. Ever
when its terms are counted obsolete, its essential truth remains
and the Church's duty is one of constant re-examination and re
interpretation of that truth and its relevance for the life of to-day
A living faith both abides and grows; abides because it grows
unfolds, expands, taking all the forms that life and power take
Yet it is ever the same in its essence, in its central insight and attach
ment. Faith must of necessity grow, by its own inner spiritual logic
It is real only when it does grow. He who has a living faith wil
recognize that faith in new forms and patterns. Indeed every mai

supplies the true test of his own faith. A living faith always modernizes itself as of necessity it must, brings itself up to date, catches the newest phase of the Divine movement. The *truth* of dogma may be static without being stagnant, permanent but not petrified, since the *faith* which it expresses is a spring with infinite summers in its soul. It has always more harvests to give and more worlds to conquer. 'He appeared unto them *in another form*' is a text of which the whole of Christian history is an exegesis.

True religion is not a rare exotic, or a talisman, to be sought far and wide: it is the 'spirit of truth' nigh to man, even to his heart. Let a man dare to trust and obey what he sincerely believes to be the highest, truest, noblest, best, most God-like, and he will inevitably come to Christ in the experience of a fellowship dearer than life itself. Nothing could be simpler, more natural, or nearer the heart of man to do: for this is the true life, and the way to it is the Christ-way. Modern psychology, probing below the conscious surface, fails to discover any of its unprepossessing reasons for his being a Christian in thought, word, and deed.

The Church's dogmas, therefore, are but the expression of men's haunting hopes, clarifying what otherwise is vague in their minds and what so few are able to express in lucid language. But men still reject them as being remote from actual life, artificial and unreal, which fail to interpret men to themselves and are, at least for educated men, wrongly articulated. Yet, like Pharaoh, our humanity is visited by a mysterious Dream of things eternal, and is sorely troubled by it. Soothsayers and so-called Wise Men read the meaning of the Dream according to their interest or their ignorance, guessing at its omens. The need is, as of old, for the Interpreter; and the only One who has most clearly set forth the meaning of the Dream is Christ. And the meaning is seen to have cosmic significance and implication, since for every single soul He makes the eternal truth of God of such paramount importance that every man's spirit might speak His voice and live His truth. In every soul there is something unique, particular, precious, for whom Christ must be seen as the Cosmic Christ; for if our modern world is not to collapse by reason of its own disintegrating forces, it is to the Universal Christ that we must turn for world-salvation, *now*, in the tiny arc of to-day as well as in the larger cycle of time. He is the Fulfiller and Fulfilment of God's Eternal Intention

for our world; and not only for the world at large, but also for
every man born into the world. In other words, Christ must be
the centre of every man's spiritual solar system, contemplating
the results which come from a true and steadily maintained orbit
It is the Eternal Christ, yet the Outcast Christ, so long despised and
rejected of men, the Saviour who 'sorrows with indomitable eyes,'
yet hoping all things, believing all things, even whilst enduring all
things, the Crucified Redeemer, to whom the world must turn
for the true sanity of life; the Risen, Ascended and Reigning Christ
to whom all power is given in earth and heaven; the Cosmic Christ
whom our humanity will one day crown without a thorn, His
spirit our salvation, His love the life of every soul, His law the
only basis of a world-order wherein dwelleth righteousness and
peace. But not the least aspect of our modern heresy is the pinning
of our faith to the provisions of a Welfare State run by Boards of
Control and multitudes of Civil Servants; whilst not a few folk
are prone to believe that the future of mankind will be a Marxist
millennium with communist Colonies established on every planet.
Yet, however far man may go in such directions he will still be man:
unable to escape from himself, he will take with him that sinful
self which needs redemption. Where will redemption be found
except in Christ who, in the light of modern need and future
development, increasingly becomes the Cosmic Christ. Meanwhile,
man-made Paradises which look so alluring on paper not infre-
quently turn out to be Police States and Concentration Camps, but
never a City with Foundations whose Builder and Maker is God.

Had Paul given us no word beyond Romans 5 [20], he would yet
have stated one of the profoundest truths in the universe: 'Where
sin abounded, grace did abound yet more exceedingly.' In this
phrase he has put his finger with an immortal touch on the vital
secret of all true hope, and has shown us, what a superficial knowledge of human experience might have rendered doubtful, that
Heaven is always on the winning side. Temporary failures, such
as we of our generation have so bitterly experienced, may seem to
prove the contrary, so that we look fearfully upon the dreaded
possibility of the annihilation of a world whose roots appear all too
certainly to be established in evil. But the humiliation passes,
and the world endures. The something of Heaven has held its own
against the something of Earth. In the matching of unequal anti-

theses Heaven must ultimately win, because grace is 'over and above more than enough,' as the strong, significant, untranslatable Greek word has it (ὑπερπερισσεύω), and grace stands side by side with sin; each is the implication of the other. The Pauline injunction to 'fight the good fight of faith' (1 *Tim.* 6 [12]) is thus a promise as well as a command. Faith is an essential element in this warfare, because the issue is not yet; but only 'not yet' with regard to the human plane; on the Divine plane the end is assured; for Paul goes on to urge: 'lay hold on eternal life,' because our hope is in the eternal, not the temporal: therefore make your own by an all-out effort of the whole man what already is in the Being of God; make real that whereunto you are called; make actual what is potential: do not be daunted by the clash and the conflict. The 'Everlasting Yea' proceeds out of faith as a starting-point to ever fuller heights. Faith is the great condition of the aspirant after Christlikeness. 'Christhood' is Paul's objective, the alpha and omega of his Epistles, the great text that flames across every fervid page: the Christhood of the Master, the like promise for those who are 'joint-heirs with Him.' Hence that resounding keynote of Christhood, καταλλαγή (*Rom.* 5 [8-11]), at-one-ment, reconciliation, offered through Jesus to us, and offered as an expression of the Everlasting Love, and not of wrath, of Him who thus 'commendeth His love to us while we were yet sinners.' The putting away of sin, the bringing nigh of them that were far off, the restoration of a fallen consciousness, the affirmation of a new, a spiritual, day that was to dawn over the horizon of an already far-spent night: these things were all involved in the great Ideal, these the burden of an optimism which has no superior in the world of religious thought.

So, after ages of tragedy, we come with bleeding feet to learn that in Christ Jesus the Voice of the universe found its most authentic expression, and that there is neither stability nor security until we obey His word which provides the only hope of a world that we vainly trusted would have been made wiser by its folly and nobler by its suffering. Well may we pray for the reign of the Cosmic Christ, and look for the day when the vast invisible spiritual world will break in upon the visible and material order to transform and glorify it, and Christ be All in all.